live at 5

The Story
Behind Its Success

Steve Murphy

NIMBUS
PUBLISHING

The author's share of proceeds from the sale of this book will be donated to Christmas Daddies and the IWK Hospital for Children.

Nimbus Publishing Limited
PO Box 9166
Halifax, NS   B3K 5M8
(902) 455-4286

Printed and bound in Canada
Design: Kathy Kaulbach, Paragon Design Group
Front and back cover photo by Steve Townsend

National Library of Canada Cataloguing in Publication

Murphy, Steve
Live at 5 / Steve Murphy.
ISBN 1-55109-412-6

1. Live at 5 (Television program). I. Title. II. Title: Live at five.

PN1992.77.L59M87 2002   791.45'72   C2002-903460-4

Canada   The Canada Council | Le Conseil des Arts
          for the Arts | du Canada

We acknowledge the financial support of the Government of Canada through the Book Publishing Industry Development Program (BPIDP) and the Canada Council for our publishing activities.

For my families, personal and professional, especially Nora, Brendan, and Jocelyn, and to the memories of Kevin MacDonald and Joe Irvine.

Table of Contents

Acknowledgements

I AM INDEBTED TO MY COLLEAGUES Wade Keller, Julie Caswell, and Leo Carter, and my former producers, Pat Krauskopf and Kristen Tynes, for putting up with my fanciful fits of writing. Nancy Regan, Ian Morrison, and Harris Sullivan helped colour in the details of my otherwise sketchy memories, and offered more than a few memories of their own. ATV vice president and general manager Mike Elgie and news director Jay Witherbee have offered enthusiastic support for the project from the moment they heard about it. Nimbus publisher Dorothy Blythe graciously accepted a manuscript from a first-time author, and my editor, Sandra McIntyre, gently and effectively polished it for publication. My friend Brian Giffin and his staff at Atlantic Photo were of enormous help with the images, most of which were shot by ATV photographers Steve Townsend and Paul Stone. "I.T." whiz Christine Norman helped with preparation of the text. Finally and most importantly, my wife and colleague, Jocelyn Murphy, has endured years of talk about this book and its contents. During innumerable and interminable conversations, her effective fact-checking and editing have been invaluable. Thank you.

Image Sources

ATV: pages 4, 5, 7, 8, 11, 15, 19, 21, 22, 23, 24, 28, 30, 31, 34, 40, 43, 44, 53, 54, 55, 57, 60, 61, 65, 72(upper), 73, 74, 79, 80, 81, 82, 85, 86, 89, 91(left), 92, 95, 97, 99, 111, 113, 114, 115, 117, 119, 120, 131, 135, 138, 139, 141, 142, 143, 145, 148, 152, 153, 154, 155, 156, 157, 158, 159, 161, 165, 173, 179, 180, 181, 182, 183, 184, 185, 189, 191, 192(upper)
ATV Christmas Daddies: pages 20, 64, 72(lower), 175, 177, 192(lower)
ATV Staff Association: pages 13, 48, 49, 150, 160, 186, 190, 194
Campbell, Mark: page 133
CJCH Radio Archive: page 47
Kay, Jonathan: page 118
Kipis, Sandra: page 149
Murphy Collection: pages 26, 66
Murphy, Douglas: pages 63, 105
Regan, Nancy: pages 91, 109, 110
Sullivan, Harris: page 56
Worrall, Bob: page 90

Foreword

FIRST AT FIVE

IT TOOK ME A LONG TIME TO READ STEVE MURPHY'S *LIVE AT 5*. With each turn of a page I had to stop and reflect. So many memories. What Steve chronicles here was, for me, the best of times with the best of friends. With each name, there's a story to be told. With the listing of assignments came recollections of faraway places, intriguing people, moments of danger, boredom, and creative satisfaction. But my reflections burned brightest when Steve writes of those who graced the ATV newsroom. All of them—and I mean all of them, whether in front or behind the camera...no exceptions—were an exceptional group of dedicated professionals who laughed, argued, and yelled a great deal. News Director Dick Prat and I had many disagreements, some of them downright ugly. However, I can't count the number of times during my tenure that Dick went to bat for me with the upstairs suits to push through one of my story ideas. Mark Campbell and I also squared off on several occasions over creative differences and there were occasions when our relationship came close to the breaking point. But, without question, Mark was an outstanding producer, especially in the field; in Berlin during the collapse of the wall, in Holland when we were tracking dope dealers, and in Gibraltar and Cairo during the Gulf War—just to mention a few—he saved me from a great deal of embarrassment and saved the company from losing a barrel of money. He was dedicated to getting the programme on the air by whatever means necessary—and there are some interesting stories there, I can tell you.

Despite the differences and the disagreements between us, our objective was always to produce the most informative and entertaining news programme in the Maritimes and beyond. We were a close family and that was obvious every night at five o'clock. For all of us, the ATV newsroom was—and continues to be—a creative utopia.

Let me point out that Steve is far too generous in his telling of my contribution to the development of *Live at 5,* in part because of what I call the "Ed Sullivan premise." Sullivan produced and hosted the most popular and long-lasting variety show in television history. He had the knack of surrounding himself with the best of talent, but all he did on air was introduce the acts. Still, without fail, the next morning everyone was asking, "Did you see *The Ed Sullivan Show* last night? That guy with the doves was..." They talked about the acts but Sullivan got the credit. And so it was with *Live at 5*. I was the producer, host, and the face, sure, but it was the other talent that made the show: the reporters, camerapeople, editors, and studio technicians were, and still are, the heart of the programme.

Finally, I would add to Steve's journal what he would not write himself about the number of times he carried me through difficult times on air. I'm a storyteller. I need time to research and assemble the story. That's why any victories I may have had are documentaries or programmes that I had time to work on and present later. I find reporting on politics boring and, with the exception of interviewing the newsmakers and following certain causes, I have little interest in it. Steve, on the other hand, has a quick mind that draws from an amazing database of facts, figures, and names, coupled with an insatiable thirst for political history and stories of backroom haggling. He could ad lib his way into a Bin Laden cave. I can't count the number of times Dick Prat had the good sense to make sure Steve was by my side when we covered "live" elections or historical events together.

The story of *Live at 5* is a great read because it is about people you have generously invited into your homes on a regular basis over the years. Some you know, others you'll be interested in meeting for the first time. This is a story about a news programme that has won favour because the news people who produce it and the viewers who support it all live in the Maritime neighbourhood. Thanks, Steve, for telling our story, and here's to family.

Dave Wright

Introduction

MIKE ELGIE HAD GOOD REASON TO SMILE as he strode through the ATV Newscentre. ATV's youthful vice-president and general manager was holding the latest ratings from the Bureau of Broadcast Measurement (BBM).

"Great book," he beamed, in reference to the audience numbers for *Live at 5* and *The ATV Evening News* just published by the BBM. (Once published in books the size of telephone directories, these ratings reports are now delivered online.) It was January 2002 and the ratings for ATV's flagship shows had seldom been better—a noteworthy accomplishment in the so-called "five-hundred-channel universe," in which audiences have shrunk as the number of alternatives has exploded.

Maritimers are inveterate television news viewers. We watch more news broadcasts than almost anyone else in Canada. And for most of the last twenty years, the news programmes we have watched have been on ATV. In recent years, *Live at 5* and *The ATV Evening News* have been the most popular of all the programmes on television...even in the five-hundred-channel world.

This is the story of ATV News and *Live at 5,* a programme so much a part of the fabric of Maritime life that its name has become part of the local lexicon. It's been the subject of skits by the late, great Cape Breton Summertime Revue, the punchline for stand-up comic Tony Quinn, and the object of parody. But mostly, it's been watched by no less than a quarter of a million people a day, practically since its inception in 1982.

I was privileged to host and produce *Live at 5* from 1986 to 1993, after Dave Wright, before (and then with) Nancy Regan and Paul Mennier and now Ron Kronstein. My involvement with the programme dates back to its debut in 1982, when I was the show's editorial commentator. It continues today as I present the news headlines in the run-up to the ATV evening newshour.

A dozen years ago, a good friend, lawyer Gordon Proudfoot, suggested I write a book about something I know. It was a suggestion my father, Doug Murphy, never let me forget! I made the decision to write about my experiences on the show in January 1997, hoping to finish in time for *Live at 5's* fifteenth anniversary in the fall of that year. I was both naïve and far too ambitious—since that day in 1997 it has taken a few minutes a day, every other day to produce a presentable draft.

This book attempts to answer virtually every question I have ever been asked about *Live at 5,* particularly the ones I am asked most often. This is life at five.

The Wright Stuff

THE CALL TO THE PHONE CAME AS A WELCOME ESCAPE from the blistering heat. It was mid-July in 1986 and I was battling the weeds in back of my home on Halifax's Robie Street. The sun was shining and the weeds were winning, so the telephone call from Dick Prat did not seem even remotely like an intrusion. I was shocked by what he had to say.

"Dave Wright is going to Boston. He's leaving as soon as possible, so I need you to start filling in right away." Dick didn't sound like a man who had just dropped a bombshell, but then again, he never did. After a decade running one of Canada's largest private television news operations, he wasn't one to panic, although this was perhaps the biggest problem he had ever been handed. Dave Wright was as close to irreplaceable as anyone could be. Not only was he the best-known and best-loved television personality in the Maritimes, he was also a master innovator. His programming ideas and unique style helped to father what was, by the mid-eighties, the most popular local programme on Maritime television. To many viewers Dave Wright was *Live at 5*. Dick Prat could not imagine the programme without the magnetic "Boomer" at the helm, and he

DAVE WRIGHT was "the Maritimes' best-known and best-loved television personality" when he announced his move to Boston in July 1986.

worried that some of the people who watched the show might not accept anyone else.

Dave Wright had come to the Maritimes ten years earlier at the behest of his long-time friend and boss Fred Sherratt. At the time, Dave was already famous in southern Ontario as the sports voice on Toronto's CHUM radio. His distinctive sign off, "Daaaaaave Wright, CHUM Sports," and his clever nickname for the Toronto Maple Leafs—"The Buds"—became part of the local lexicon. While it isn't certain that Dave Wright coined the Leafs' "diminutive" handle, as the sportscaster on the city's dominant pop radio station, he had, at the very least, popularized it. Somehow, Sherratt prevailed on Dave to take on some missionary work on the East Coast.

CHUM Limited's Halifax radio station, CJCH, needed a host for its midday phone-in show. Although he was "from away," Sherratt knew exactly the sort of person that would work in the Maritimes. And he knew the market: he got his start in broadcasting as an announcer at radio station CKCL in Truro, Nova Scotia in 1948. He returned to Nova Scotia seventeen years later

ATV PRESIDENT
Fred Sherratt, the
man who brought
Dave Wright to
the Maritimes.

as vice-president and general manager of CJCH Radio in Halifax, when the station was purchased by Allan Waters' burgeoning CHUM Limited.

Allan Waters was a radio trailblazer who in May of 1957 gave Canada its first twenty-four-hour-a-day rock and roll radio station, the legendary 1050-CHUM Toronto. Around the same time, young Fred Sherratt co-founded radio station CFRS in Simcoe, Ontario. A few years later, Sherratt was recruited by Waters to operate his new station in Peterborough, Ontario.

By the mid-seventies, Sherratt, by then a senior executive in the CHUM organization, believed Dave Wright was just what the Halifax station needed. And after some arm-twisting, (the details of which neither man has ever revealed), Dave agreed to come to Halifax—for a year. He was an instant hit. Haligonians quickly connected with his good-natured and avuncular manner and the ratings soared. CJCH was winning the battle for listeners with its perpetual cross-town radio rival CHNS. Dave's midday programme, following on the heels of Brian Phillips' powerhouse morning show, gave the station the one-two punch it needed to dominate the Halifax radio market. Leaving the programme after a year was probably never a serious option for Dave, who was by then a bona fide radio star.

Talk show host was Dave Wright's seventh or eighth incarnation in a broadcasting career that began in the early 1950s. At one time or another, Dave had spun the discs, read the news, called play-by-play hockey, sold commercials, and even managed a radio station. At one time, he operated a consulting business, selling his expertise to other broadcasters, but he returned to on-air work in 1972 as sports director at CHUM Radio. Dave replaced a young man named Brian Williams, who left the radio station shortly after covering the historic 1972 summit series between Canada and the Soviet Union. Williams is now the lead anchor of CBC Television Sports.

Four years later, Halifax must have seemed much like Moscow to Dave and Audrey Wright. Much of it was still old and dingy; a massive downtown re-development was just beginning. It was a damp and foggy place and it was a very long way from home. The winters were drier and the summers sunnier in Barrie, but Dave's reception in the Maritimes couldn't have been warmer. Almost immediately, he was embraced by listeners usually openly suspicious of "CFAs"—"come-from-aways" in the local idiom, with "away" being anywhere other than here.

Dave established a reputation as a man with a big heart and a generous laugh. People phoned his "Action Line" with their problems, and action is what they got. Dave took on tough cases and lost causes—consumer problems and welfare battles—winning friends and admirers with every case. It was only a matter of time before the radio star was drawn to television.

Dave wasn't exactly new to the game; he had been on-air in the early days of TV and had even experimented with some novel ideas: in an early audition for Barrie's CKVR TV, he walked around the set instead of sitting behind the orange crates that doubled as a desk. This "walking and talking" style later

DAVE WRIGHT with Cathy Reardon (left) and Anne Tulloch on the set of ATV's newsmagazine *I-D* (In-Depth) in the late 1970s.

became Dave's trademark. He returned to the small screen in the late seventies on ATV's *I-D*, which was eventually reinvented and renamed *The Notebook*. It was Atlantic Canada's first supper-hour magazine show, and likely one of the first of its kind in Canada. *The Notebook* was essentially stories about what Dave Wright felt people were interested in: local news, celebrities, royalty, movie stars, amazing animals, and health issues. Many of the items were unabashedly lifted directly from American morning shows, which had almost no audience in the Maritimes. Dave did not apologize to those who thought the subject matter too light, too trivial, or too American. And there was nothing light or trivial about the ratings. Airing at five-thirty, *The Notebook* quickly garnered a legion of loyal viewers, most of whom stayed tuned for *The ATV Evening News* at six o'clock. ATV programming chief Joe Irvine and Dick Prat, who had presided over the development of *The Notebook*, had a hit on their hands. Before long, it was airing across the Maritimes, marking the beginning of ATV's successful foray into regional news.

DAVE WRIGHT'S *NOTEBOOK*, the forerunner of *Live at 5*. (Note *Hogan's Heroes* in the far left monitor, and President Jimmy Carter in the centre.)

The Notebook was also the seed from which *Live at 5* eventually sprouted. Not only was Dave Wright the show's popular front man, he was also a critical element behind the scenes from the very beginning. So, in 1986, when word got out that he was leaving the station and the region, it was big news. And a big worry for Dick Prat.

Creative Forces

THE ATLANTIC TELEVISION SYSTEM (ATV) had been born in September 1972, the child of a happy marriage of good business and good sense. In its infancy, ATV really was a system, a network created with the linking of three popular local television stations: CJCH Halifax, CKCW Moncton, and CJCB Sydney. Begun as CBC affiliates, the Sydney and Moncton operations were two of the oldest television stations in the Maritimes: CJCB Sydney signed-on on October 9, 1954, followed by CKCW Moncton less than two months later. Both remained CBC affiliates until their acquisition by CHUM Limited in 1969 and 1972 respectively. CJCH Halifax was the new kid on the block. Founded in 1961 by a group headed by broadcasting pioneer Finlay Macdonald, the station was one of the original members of CTV when the new national network flickered into existence in 1962. When CHUM purchased the Halifax television station in 1971, it got equity in the CTV network (really more like an owner-operated co-operative) as part of the bargain. CHUM's three Maritime stations were then affiliated with the national network of which CHUM was an owner.

Allan Waters and Fred Sherratt quickly recognized the opportunity the stations presented. Each boasted an expansive system of transmitters which, when combined, provided off-air television signals to virtually all of the populated Maritimes. Putting the three stations together as a regional network could obviously improve the bottom line; at the same time, the quality of local programming, especially news programmes, would be enhanced. Sherratt chose veteran broadcaster Joe Irvine to oversee the merger.

A New Brunswick native, Joe Irvine had experience in news, sales, and programming. He spent many years with Fred Lynd's *Lionel Television* (CKCW), and was a natural choice to become vice-president of programming for the new ATV system. Marven Nathanson, who had bartered his interest in CJCB-TV for shares in the new venture, moved to Halifax as vice-president of operations, while the affable Ken Boyce ran the advertising and sales side of things from CJCB in Sydney. Marven and his brother Norris retained their interest in the family business, operating CJCB Radio and its FM sibling.

Initially, each ATV station retained its news staff and local news programme, but began sharing stories of regional interest. Dick Prat's combined television-radio newsroom in Halifax was the largest of the three, so it came as little surprise that he was eventually chosen to oversee the regional news operation. The CJCH radio and television newsrooms were separated in 1978, leaving Dick to envision a regional future for the ATV system.

The promotion capped a meteoric rise for Dick. Only a dozen years earlier, the young man from Bridgetown, Nova Scotia, was getting coffee for the more exalted members of the CJCH news staff. The pesky youngster had been hired as a studio hand at the new television station, but was drawn to the radio side, where he fell under the spell of seasoned reporters the likes of Mike Duffy, Max Keeping, and Harris Sullivan. They were breaking stories and making waves, and it wasn't long before Dick was raking some muck of his own as a streetwise reporter. Always outspoken, even abrasive, he was also loudly lamenting the lack of direction in the otherwise energetic newsroom of the sixties.

THE FOUNDING FATHERS of ATV, from left to right, vice-presidents Joe Irvine, Marven Nathanson, and Ken Boyce, ATV president Fred Sherratt, and CHUM Limited's last general manager at ATV, Greg Mudry.

"He wasn't wrong," Harris Sullivan recalls, "and before we knew it, the notice went up on the [bulletin] board that we were all working for the little bugger."

Harris was something of a whiz-kid himself. Only twenty-one years old when he arrived at CJCH Halifax in 1961, the Richibucto, New Brunswick, native had already had a six-year career in newspapers, including a two-year stint as a news editor at *The Moncton Times*. At that time, he was the youngest news editor at a daily newspaper in Canada. Although he would later play a significant role himself, Harris is quick to credit Dick with both the vision and the efficient determination that led to ATV's hugely successful foray into regional programming. While few would argue with the clarity and farsightedness of Dick's vision, he developed a reputation for hard-headedness, and wasn't above cajoling his colleagues and others to get his way. Whatever the technique, Harris says Dick was a master motivator. Among his staff he was known as a man who drove hard bargains but always kept his word. His instincts about news and regional television programming speak for themselves.

Although Dave Wright's *Notebook* represented the first step down the long road leading to a regional newscast, even it was not totally regional. Several minutes of each programme were devoted to local news, read by announcers in Sydney, Moncton, and Saint John. Dave hosted the rest of the show, and quickly became just as popular on evening television as he was on morning radio. Before long, Joe and Dick agreed that Dave should also move into prime time. *The Wright Time* was a half-hour interview show that featured Maritimers from all walks of life in conversation with the congenial Dave. The weekly exposure in prime time helped make Dave Wright a household name across the Maritimes, and the only logical person to quarterback the big play that was coming.

I first met Dave Wright on May 13, 1980. It was my brother Peter's seventeenth birthday and my first day on the job at CJCH radio. I had given up the security of reading morning news on CFBC, in my hometown of Saint John, in favour of the afternoon news run in Halifax. My friend Rick Howe had made the move a year earlier and had convinced me to do the same. The station, the city, and the dollars were all bigger. Part of my duties as afternoon editor involved writing local news copy for Dave Wright's *Noon Report*, the most widely listened-to midday newscast in the Maritimes. Dave selected and wrote most of the material himself after he signed off his phone-in show at 11:00 A.M., but he preferred that local stories came from the newsroom.

Writing for Dave was an education. He didn't care for traditional, "dull" news copy. He liked stories that were written for the way he read news, which was pretty much the way he spoke. Also, Dave was prone to mispronouncing names, so phonetic spelling was called for—"Dunna-who" for Donahoe and "Muska-dob-it" for Musquodoboit, for example.

The Noon Report was a lot like *The Notebook*, heavy on celebrity news, medical stories, and humorous "believe it or not" material, with the top local stories told in Dave's folksy, conversational style. It became my duty to write them that way, a task which ultimately affected the way I read and write news myself. To say that Dave Wright was a role model is a serious

DICK PRAT, in his
mid-thirties when
chosen to run
one of Canada's
largest private
television news
operations.

understatement. He ultimately became my mentor, benefactor, and friend.

I didn't know it, but by the time I arrived at CJCH, Dave was already itching to move to television full time. He had made good on his one-year commitment to Fred Sherratt four times over, and Dick Prat was anxious to secure the full-time services of his biggest star. Besides, Dave wanted to take the TV show on the road, but was constrained by his daily radio commitment. Sherratt was willing to allow Dave out of the radio deal but first he needed to find a replacement host for the popular *Hotline* programme. I had had some experience behind the mike of a phone-in show, substitute hosting on occasion for the irascible Tom Young on CFBC's long-running *Talk of the Town* show. Whether Dave knew about my experience, I still don't know, but I was tapped to fill in for him one morning on *Hotline*. I had already read *The Noon Report* on a number of occasions, and before long I was Dave's designated replacement on the phone-in show, too. In this, Dave was particularly supportive, and made no secret of the fact that he saw me as somewhat integral to his plan to move to television.

In the fall of 1981, CJCH manager Bill Bodnarchuk and news director Chuck Bridges took the plunge and moved me into the *Hotline* hotseat; Dave moved down the hall and around the corner to a permanent, full-time position in the ATV newsroom. The transition might have been difficult had it not been for Dave's willingness to make it work. He not only supported the move publicly, but also offered as much personal support as I could have wanted. He shared his keen insight into what made *Hotline* work and offered advice anytime I sought it. It was to be the first of three occasions on which I had the good fortune to inherit a popular programme from the Boomer.

Around the same time, Dick Prat began the search for an executive producer to oversee his growing news empire. By now, *The ATV Evening News* was a single programme, hosted from Halifax by the experienced and well-respected Bruce Graham, who had returned to the Maritimes after several years in Western Canada. *The Notebook* continued to be an unbeatable "lead in" to the crucial six o'clock period, when ATV went head-to-head with CBC News. At that time, sixty minutes of news was a rarity in private television—"a hungry beast," according to Harris Sullivan, who had left ATV in 1974 for the CBC. But if an hour-long programme was hungry, a ninety-minute programme would be insatiable. And ninety minutes is exactly what Dick Prat had in mind when he hired his old friend Harris Sullivan to return to the private sector.

Harris Sullivan was and is a legendary figure in Halifax broadcasting. Outspoken and outgoing, he set the staid Nova Scotia capital on its ear in the mid-sixties with his frank, irreverent style. He once started a newscast on CJCH Radio with a headline proclaiming: "Jesus Christ may have been homosexual." (The story dealt with an offbeat claim made by an unknown theologian of dubious qualification. But the headline is what everyone remembered!) As a sportscaster, Harris called them as he saw them, frequently dubbing some sports hero or another the "goat of the week." Haligonians later put a face to the name when Harris moved to television as one of the principals on CJCH TV's *I-D* supper-hour news programme.

THE DYNAMIC DUO—ATV's unbeatable 1980 anchor team: Dave Wright at 5:30 and Bruce Graham (left) at 6:00 P.M.

Harris's off-camera escapades were also well known, and in that he was not alone. A motley band of characters on both sides of the camera worked hard to turn out a popular and controversial programme, and when it was over, some of them played just as hard. Today, Sullivan cites Edmund Morris, the news editorialist on the radio and television stations (and later mayor of Halifax and a long-serving provincial cabinet minister), as the moral and ethical compass that kept the otherwise wild and crazy place intact.

It was during this golden era, with its irrepressible on-air personalities and their colourful off-air exploits, that Dick Prat arrived on the scene. Dick and Harris were to become fast friends and trusted colleagues. Harris spent several years reporting and producing at CBC Halifax. But in 1981, when Dick Prat found himself looking for a lieutenant to command his growing newsroom, he knew he could trust the job to his old friend Harris Sullivan.

Jim Nunn, the lanky former anchor of the local news on CBC Halifax and my ex-brother-in-law, is fond of claiming that it was he who conceived of ATV's move into regional newscasting.

Nunn, now host of the popular national programme
Marketplace, worked for Dick Prat briefly in the 1970s, reporting from ATV's Ottawa bureau. While he and Dick undoubtedly discussed the concept of a regional newscast several years
before it happened, the idea likely germinated with the forma-
tion of ATV. What was not determined until much later was the
precise form the regional newscast would take. Although Dave
Wright's style and personality were significant factors in the
format ultimately chosen, a man named Jacques DeSuze also
had more than a little to do with it.

Jacques DeSuze grew up in the media. His father, Carl, was
a legendary figure at Boston's WBZ Radio. The young Jacques
was what we in the business call "a news doctor," a euphemism
for "news consultant." From his headquarters at the McHugh
and Hoffman consulting group in Washington DC, Jacques travelled the world, marketing his ideas on how to create and
improve news programmes. A by-product of this travel was that
Jacques got to watch a lot of television. He saw what worked
and what didn't, borrowed what he liked, modified it, then recommended it to other stations. In the early eighties, Jacques
noticed that, in New York, hour-long,early evening news magazine programmes were working. Few stations (none in Canada,
Harris Sullivan believes) were producing five o'clock newscasts at that time, but with ATV blazing a bold new trail with a
successful show at five-thirty, Dick Prat figured a five o'clock
programme was the next natural step. Fred Sherratt and Joe
Irvine knew the value of locally produced Canadian programming (it's also a condition attached to a broadcasting license,
then and now), and supported the idea. Jacques contributed suggestions about content and style, many of which mirrored what
Dave Wright wanted to do. Most importantly, it was Jacques
who offered up the name for the new programme. On ATV, as
on WNBC New York, the early evening news would be called
"Live at 5."

Jacques also played a pivotal creative role in the development
of Toronto television station CITY-TV, also owned by CHUM.
(It was there that Jacques met Fred Sherratt, who dispatched

him to Halifax.) Just how much credit he gets for the "uptown," no-studio style of production now synonymous with CITY depends on who you talk to. Moses Znaimer, the visionary founder of the station, usually reserves the lion's share of the plaudits for himself. Others see Jacques as the co-creator of the CITY style, at the very least. Regardless of who you believe, one fact speaks for itself: when CHUM decided to market and license CITY-TV's unique style to the world, the man they recruited to run CHUMCity International was none other than Jacques DeSuze.

The Hungry Beast

HARRIS SULLIVAN'S "HUNGRY BEAST" would require a lot of care and feeding. In fact, it was more than his existing news staff could handle. For one thing, Dick Prat didn't want to run an hour of recycled American news between five and six o'clock. He knew that Hollywood profiles, medical stories, and news features would remain an important part of his new news-magazine, but he wanted to give the programme a strong Maritime flavour, and make it a showcase for ATV's best journalists and the station's growing technical acumen. Dick saw the "live" in *Live at 5* as crucial to the new programme's success. He knew that although Dave Wright would be the main attraction, sec-ondary players would be needed to make the hour-long pro-gramme work. A newsmagazine needed "columns," and Harris and Dick designed the *Live at 5* format to include several.

Jacques deSuze had identified consumer issues as an area of growing importance to news viewers. Many American news-magazines had consumer reporters in featured roles, and Dick and Harris decided to do the same. Debi Forsyth-Smith had been producing ATV's mid-morning news programme, *Atlantic AM,* for several years when she was tapped to become the consumer

Live at 5 weather
anchor and
environment
reporter
Susan Dunn.

reporter on *Live at 5*. Halifax-based financial planner Dave Salmon, who had been dispensing advice on CJCH Radio's *Hotline* programme, came to television a short time later, counseling "it is your money, manage it wisely."

Although weather forecaster Susan Dunn was already appearing on *The ATV Evening News,* her role was expanded to include some environmental stories and more detailed forecasts on *Live at 5*. Sportscaster Paul Lethbridge was given extra time in the hour-long programme, and was encouraged to showcase "Sports Extras"—stories from the world of sports with a wide viewer appeal.

Dick and Harris decided the newsmagazine needed a daily editorial commentary and occasional letters to the editor. The colourful and controversial Dick Smyth was producing daily opinion pieces for CHUM's CITY-TV in Toronto, but because some of the pieces were national in nature they could work for a Maritime audience as well. But Dick and Harris also wanted local and regional commentaries, and that's where I came in. As host of a phone-in show, I was already recognized in the Halifax area as an opinion broadcaster. My radio chores were wrapped

"Here's how
things look to
Dick Smyth...."
Live At 5's
Toronto-based
national
commentator
Dick Smyth with
ATV news
director Dick
Prat.

up by one o'clock daily, so I had ample opportunity to write and
videotape a television commentary on short notice. And as a
New Brunswicker living and working in Nova Scotia, I was
familiar with the stories and issues of ATV's two principal markets. Steve Murphy, commentator, made his debut the day the
new programme premiered—September 13, 1982.

The new programme had its share of skeptics, including a few
at ATV who worried the place was going to burst at the seams,
cranking out ninety minutes of news everyday. And if that
weren't enough, ATV was preparing to launch its second signal, ATV2, six months later. The Atlantic Satellite Network, as
the service was later renamed, would be producing its own news
programmes at 7:00 P.M. and 11:00 P.M., from a set at the opposite end of the ATV news studio. Ron Kronstein, Carole McDade,
Duane Lowe, and Scott Matthews were hired to produce and host
the shows, and veteran radio newsman Daryl Good was brought
in as a writer. The remaining resources were drawn from ATV's
already over-worked production staff. On May 29, 1983, from a
set opposite the *ATV Evening News* desk, the cameras spun
around 180 degrees to shoot the first *Atlantic Pulse*.

STEVE MURPHY, 1982. On radio by day, TV by night!

ATLANTIC PULSE. The original anchor team on ATV's second signal, ASN. Left to right, Duane Lowe, Ron Kronstein, Carol McDade, and sportscaster Scott Mathews (wearing jeans!)

Sitting *on* the
desk, not behind
it, was Dave
Wright's *Live at
5* trademark.

The public took to *Live at 5* almost immediately. Viewers
liked the content and the programme's polished appearance.
ATV was using a so-called "working newsroom," where the
news is prepared in the same room it is broadcast from. This
arrangement became popular in the 1990s, but in the early eighties it was revolutionary. Even more notable was the way Dave
Wright moved around the newsroom, casually walking up to
reporters and his co-hosts, asking them what they were working on. Nor was it unusual for Dave to sit on the edge of a desk
instead of behind it. And Dave didn't really read the news, he
spoke it, punctuating the patter with conversational expressions,
including "our Maritime neighbourhood," which became the
way Dave chose to define ATV's extended-coverage area. A
neighbourhood is what, in reality, ATV's market was becoming.
A regional newscast with stories from Halifax, Sydney,
Moncton, Saint John, and all points in between, the show fos-
tered a broad community of interest based more on issues than
on geography. Maritimers began to realize they had a great deal
in common, that what mattered in one corner of the region was
of interest and often of importance in another.

STEVE MURPHY
AND NANCY
REGAN in a 1991
TV Guide cover
story.

And then there were the "Staytogethers." *Live at 5* began to broadcast wedding anniversary announcements, culminating with the couple who had been together the longest—"the Champion Staytogethers." This feature, introduced as a way to fill time with "nice news," generated an overwhelming response: marital longevity was something Maritimers valued and *Live at 5* reflected that. The anniversary announcements are still a part of *Live at 5* everyday. The idea of broadcasting marriage milestones, complete with still photographs and family statistics, flies in the face of what passes for good programming in the rest of the television world, but it works in the Maritime neighbourhood.

In an interview for a 1991 *TV Guide* cover story, Nancy Regan and I were questioned at length about the marriage milestones. The implication was that the feature was, at the very least, hokey, at the worst, bad television. We explained that *Live at 5* was, at least in part, a celebration of accomplishments, and that in the Maritimes being married for fifty years or longer was something people were proud of—rightly so. Plus, people married for such a long time tend to have large families and legions

"For 'Consumerwatch,' I'm Debi
Forsyth-Smith." Debi was
Live at 5's first consumer reporter.

of friends; in a business that's about giving people reasons to watch, what better reason to watch could there be than the possibility of seeing someone you know?

"Interactive" and "multi-media" are two popular buzzwords in television these days, as producers search for ways to get viewers personally involved with the shows they watch. Years before the internet started collecting opinions about the pressing issues of the day, *Live at 5* was running telephone polls. In the beginning it wasn't unusual to get ten or fifteen thousand calls on a hot topic, like capital punishment. So popular were these polls that, for a time, ATV was the largest generator of "900" calls in Canada. But even with the novelty well worn off, at least a thousand Maritimers spend 63 cents a call to be heard every time *Live at 5* asks a question.

Over the years, tens of thousands of Maritimers have phoned and mailed in to contests sponsored by *Live at 5*. Many more picked up and returned "Heart Quiz" and blood pressure questionnaires. An astonishing eighty thousand people were involved in a colon-cancer early-detection promotion in the early nineties. A similar screening programme in the mid-eighties met with similar success, although it created a huge problem when some viewers mailed in inappropriately packaged "samples." Postal workers at the main sorting station in Halifax refused to handle the material. The second time we conducted the "Hemocult" programme, samples in carefully sealed, sterile packages were hand delivered directly to Shoppers Drug Mart pharmacies. The people of the Maritimes have always enjoyed the opportunity to be involved with the programme, establishing themselves as pioneers of multi-media interaction.

By the early eighties, satellites were routinely beaming pictures from the four points of the compass into the ATV newsroom and on into Maritime living rooms. Dave Wright was watching all of this with great interest. Dave loved to travel and he suspected that Maritimers would love to experience the world, so he struck upon the idea of originating a television show from some distant location. In 1981, he proposed taking *The Notebook* to London for the wedding of Prince Charles and Lady Diana Spencer. Both an experienced traveler and a clever TV producer, Dave cooked up a plan that would allow ATV to be there for the "wedding of the century" (which barely lasted the decade), at a fraction of the cost. It was the sort of plan Dick Prat appreciated most—high profile, without the high price. The secret was in the pre-production: most of the programme viewed by Maritimers on July 21, 1981, was produced a couple of weeks earlier by Dave and his advance team, which included seasoned producer Jim Hill, Sr. Jim had come to Canada from England in 1956, arriving at CJCH-TV after working for a few years as a freelance sound engineer. Jim not only knew his craft and his native country, but, having produced and directed countless episodes of the *The Wright Time* and *The Notebook,* he also knew Dave, the way he thought and the way he worked. They travelled around England with cameraman Al Eastman shooting colour (or background) stories, which were assembled back in Halifax. The day of the wedding, Dave and Jim produced *The Notebook* live-to-tape, on location in London. They used their own video, plus pictures begged and borrowed from, or swapped

ATV'S 1997 CREW, covering the funeral of the Princess of Wales. Cameraman
Paul Creelman, Steve Murphy, Technical Producer Greg Campbell, and
Producer Peter Hays at Buckingham Palace, London. Dave Wright reported
from the same location sixteen years earlier on the day of Diana's marriage to
Prince Charles.

with, ABC. In fact, Dave Wright's tiny ATV team was tapped
as a backup crew by Peter Jennings, who was at that time
anchoring the overseas portion of the ABC flagship *World News
Tonight* from London (with Frank Reynolds in Washington and
Max Robinson in Chicago). In exchange for helping ex-patriot
Jennings and company, Dave got access to ABC pictures and
editing facilities. The material was shuttled by taxi to Heathrow
and flown to Halifax, arriving just in time to be played back to
the Maritimes at five-thirty. It worked beautifully. Although no
one ever claimed that it was, the programme looked and felt
live—and it gave ATV viewers a bona fide Maritime slant on
the fairy-tale wedding. It was also a first for ATV News and a
prototype for *Live at 5* programmes to come. When I stood in
almost precisely the same location in September 1997, reporting to Maritimers on the tragic death of the princess, I could not
help but think of Dave Wright and a much happier day sixteen

THE OTHER SIDE
OF THE CAMERA.
ATV production
truck dockside.

years earlier.

Live at 5 was broadcast live from the Halifax waterfront on the blisteringly beautiful June afternoon in 1984 when *Bluenose II* led the tall ships in the splendid "Parade of Sail." The tragic sinking of *The Marques* in a storm en route to Halifax, with the loss of all hands, had marred the otherwise hugely successful event. The story had hit the ATV newsroom particularly hard, and were it not for fate, the impact might have also been deeply personal.

To prepare for coverage of the tall ships event, some of which would be broadcast nationally by CTV, Dick Prat had dispatched a crew to Bermuda, where many of the great ships were gathering. The original plan was to have veteran reporter Ian Morrison, his cameraman, and his producer sail back to Halifax on board *The Marques*. But Ian, an experienced sailor, had uneasy feelings the moment he saw *The Marques* and decided come hell or high water he would not put himself or his crew in danger. They sailed back instead on board a Polish training vessel, a decision that turned out to have saved their lives.

The announcement that Pope John Paul was to visit the

DEBI (LEFT) AND DAVE anchor one of *Live at 5's* first live remotes at the tall
ships Parade of Sail in 1984.

COAST TO COAST.
CTV's Del
Archer and Liz
Grogan anchor
national coverage
of the Parade of
Sail.

Maritimes in the summer of 1984 sparked an idea that resulted in one of *Live at 5's* finest hours. Fascinated as he was by the pope's life story, Dave Wright decided he wanted to profile the first non-Italian pontiff in half a millennium. At a time when Poland was still a communist dictatorship, it was an ambitious idea, but Dave loved a challenge, and after much cajoling of diplomats (theirs and ours), he got the green light. With passports and visas in hand, Dave and cameraman Jamie Munro were off to Poland to tell "The Story of a Pope." Before it was over, Dave found himself face to face with the pontiff in a hastily-arranged encounter at the Vatican. The photograph of their meeting is a personal favourite of Dave's and a treasured part of the history of ATV News. The programme that was ultimately produced was a remarkable and widely acclaimed piece of television that set the tone for the pope's visit.

One of the enduring images of the 1980s is that of thousands of Ethiopian children bloated with hunger and dying amid the torment of a civil war. A long drought had rendered the already poverty-stricken nation a dustbowl, but the story went largely unreported in the Western media until a British reporter was dispatched to see just how bad the situation really was. His story, with its gut-wrenching close-ups of tiny, emaciated faces, was picked up and broadcast by virtually every television news organization in the world, including ATV. Almost overnight, hundreds of journalists descended on Africa to get the story. As coverage increased, so did the number of telephone calls to relief agencies around the world. People wanted to do something about the starvation and death in Ethiopia. Maritimers, too, wanted to help and Dave Wright gave them the opportunity to do something meaningful, something that had never been done before.

It wasn't Dave's idea to adopt a village but it certainly was his enthusiasm for the project that made it happen. The Adopt-a-Village initiative grew out of the Ethiopia Airlift campaign organized in October 1984 by Peter Dalglish, a Halifax law student, and John Godfrey, then president of the University of King's College. Dave provided extensive coverage of the airlift

A TREASURED
MEMORY: Dave
Wright meets
Pope John Paul II
in Vatican City in
1984.

on *Live at 5*. Godfrey, now the Liberal Member of Parliament for the Toronto area riding of Don Valley West, credits Dave with communicating the complex situation in Africa in a straightforward way that resonated with Maritimers. *Live at 5's* huge audience was quick to respond; within weeks, food and medicine were being shipped from the Maritimes to Ethiopia. But Godfrey was not satisfied with this Band-Aid approach to the problem; he wanted to do something that would have a profound and lasting impact on the poverty and starvation in Ethiopia. As he lay awake one night wondering what more could be done, the concept of adopting a village came to him.

Dave recognized almost immediately the appeal such a project would have in the Maritimes. Through *Live at 5*, Maritimers were encouraged to donate what they could to the village of Degahabur, in the Ogaden Desert. Dave travelled to the adopted village with cameraman Dave Pike to report on the relief effort. Despite living in so-called "have-not" provinces, Maritimers responded to the Adopt-a-Village campaign by eventually contributing more than $100,000. John Godfrey insists

DAVE WRIGHT and cameraman Dave Pike visit the Ethiopian village "adopted" by Maritimers at the height of the famine in the mid-eighties.

Dave Wright deserves much of the credit: "His stories emphasized the dignity and respect of the people on the ground. He didn't patronize them…[Dave's stories] spoke to his basic humanity and his respect for someone else's culture."

A year later, when Dave returned to the village, he found there had been significant and permanent improvements in living conditions, including a well that provided a reliable source of water in an otherwise parched and dusty place. More than seventeen years later, John Godfrey says there is still contact between the Maritimes and Degahabur. In some small way, the world is a smaller place today because of what happened on *Live at 5* in the winter of 1985.

From the very beginning, *Live at 5* has been a team effort. As quarterback, Dave Wright called the plays and let others run with the ball. The viewers liked the format, and often commented on what they sensed was a family atmosphere—which is why it was a fairly serious issue when the first of the original players left the team. Paul Lethbridge was handling sports when the show signed on in September 1982. Fourteen months

later, he was back in his native Ontario. The search for a
replacement led to a young man who had come to Halifax a couple of years earlier to pursue his broadcasting career at CJCH
Radio. Paul Mennier didn't know much about sports, but he had
enthusiasm and personality galore!

Friends & Colleagues

I HAVE KNOWN PAUL MENNIER ALMOST MY ENTIRE LIFE. My parents, Fran and Doug, knew his parents, Alice and Art, for years before the two of us met in the mid-1960s in the Saint John church where Paul's mother played the organ. I was five and he was two. We didn't really see each other again until the fall of 1977 when Paul entered Saint John High School as a grade ten student. I was in grade twelve by day and holding down a radio job by night.

Paul and I became re-acquainted when he joined the high school debating team, "Equinox." I had had some success as a collegiate debater, finishing sixth at the national championships in 1977, and was a senior member of the team. The coach, a fresh-faced English teacher named Barry Harbinson (now the still fresh-faced vice-principal of SJHS), was anxious to bring in some "new blood" from the fresh crop of grade tens. Paul Mennier was a natural: quick thinking, quick talking, fast on his feet. He was a good debater who won his fair share of contests. But what he was really interested in was broadcasting.

Saint John High School had what we called a campus radio station—actually just a glorified super stereo system soldered

STEVE MURPHY'S LIFE-LONG
FRIEND and colleague Paul
Mennier, who also started his
career in radio at CFBC Saint
John.

together by a technical whiz named Harvey Nickerson. We all
thought Harvey was a genius…and we were right. He went on
to blaze exciting new technological trails in partnership with
New Brunswick's Fundy Communications, and is now a partner in a high-tech design firm in the southwestern United States.
But back in the 1970s, we were all amazed when he wired up a
couple of turntables, a microphone, and a tape player through a
control board connected to two giant speakers in the main hallway! We were on the air before and after classes and during the
noon hour. CRHS, as the station was called, played the hits
(Supertramp, Alan Parsons Project, Elton John, and Abba),
amid banter about the usual high school stuff: varsity sports
scores, the occasional controversial commentary, and the odd
bit of satire. It was a magnet for Paul, who excelled behind the
microphone, so much so that when my part-time job at CFBC
turned to a full-time job after graduation, I recommended him
as my replacement.

It was around that time that I began to look for new career
opportunities. Not that I was unhappy at CFBC—by then I was
reading news on the popular morning show hosted by the irre-

pressible Donnie "in the morning" Robertson and even doing a weekly comedy bit as "Percival Q. Pender, the precocious public service person." For those familiar with Percival—it was all Donnie's idea! He knew I did an impersonation of Saint John High School principal Dennis Knibb, an Oxford-educated Englishman with brilliant diction and a distinctive accent; he was elected to Saint John City Council in 1977. Donnie thought it would be funny to have a character read improbable public service announcements with Knibb-like delivery. Being too young to know any better, I agreed to perform the part. Percival never sounded exactly like my old principal, but he could have been his cousin. If Dennis was offended, he never said so, although Richard Thorne, my grade twelve homeroom teacher, decried the whole thing as disrespectful at least, downright rude at worst. Richard's concerns notwithstanding, the general public loved Percival who, with Donnie's coaching, found clever ways to take shots at public people (including Dennis Knibb!) without the mean-spiritedness often found in satire. So popular was the precocious Pender that when Donnie Robertson celebrated his twentieth anniversary on the air in Saint John in the late eighties, Percival was invited to make an "encore" and a final appearance.

I had intended to spend only a year in broadcasting before attending university to study journalism or law. After the first year of work, I was hopelessly hooked, although I realized a career in broadcasting would ultimately mean moving, either for a better position or a bigger paycheck, or both.

By late 1979, I was having serious discussions with "Nova Scotia's first radio station" CHNS about moving to Halifax. News Director Dave MacLachlan had invited me down to do a voice test and writing exercise, both of which I must have passed because he offered me a job reading the evening news. I was flattered but turned it down during a phone call placed from Tom Young's *Talk of the Town* studio. Dave MacLachlan and I would later become friends, even if cross-town rivals!

A few weeks later, I received a call from Ruby MacSween, general manager of CKCL Truro. She was looking for a news director, and Dave MacLachlan had recommended me. I took the train to Truro and was prepared to take the job, even going so far as to type up a letter of resignation thanking CFBC for the great start in radio, when Mark Lee suggested we have lunch. Mark was programme director at CFBC and the man largely responsible for the station's dominance of the Saint John radio ratings. He had kept the station on the air through the Great Ground Hog Gale of March 1976, during and after which most of southern New Brunswick was without power and heat. For several days CFBC was virtually the only source of information in a city on the brink of a civil disaster. Mark Lee, Tom Young, Donnie Robertson, Dave Cochrane, and other CFBC personalities were the voices of reassurance and support during those fearsome times. Saint John rewarded CFBC by continuing to listen after the power and heat came back on. By 1979 the station was unbeatable, and I was lucky enough to be part of it. Mark didn't care for the idea of my leaving the station, particularly for a much smaller market, so over a delicious meal of filet mignon, Chinese style, at the House of Chan restaurant, he suggested that I stay in Saint John for a little extra money and a lot of extra responsibility. He proposed that I assume responsibility for news on CFBC's FM station, including the production of a weekly public affairs programme and daily commentaries. It was the best of both worlds for a nineteen-year-old kid. I phoned Ruby MacSween and told her I wouldn't be going to Truro. A few months later though, when Bob Bishop called, it was a different story.

To this day, almost nobody knows who wrote the letter or sent the copies, but I was one of several dozen journalists to receive one. The letter alleged that Nova Scotia development minister Roland Thornhill had received special treatment from several of the chartered banks in the settlement of his private debts—25 cents on the dollar. One morning in the fall of 1979, I referred to the letter, without naming names, in a commentary on CFBC-FM. Through the magic of coaxial cable, Bob Bishop was listening (CFBC-FM was carried on cable in Halifax). "Bish" was news director at 92/CJCH and he was looking to hire an afternoon drive man (someone to read news on the afternoon drive home show). He liked what he heard and had Rick Howe give me a call. Rick was a friend, former colleague, and role model who had jumped to "CJ" several months earlier. These days, he hosts the phone-in show (still *The Hotline*), which is now an early afternoon show on radio station 780/KIXX. But in 1979 he was a reporter chasing "the Thornhill affair."

"So," he began, "I hear you got a letter." Rick had received a copy of the anonymous letter too, and was curious to know what, if anything, I had been able to find out about it. But that wasn't the only reason for the call. Rick thought there was a pretty good chance that I might have a shot at the afternoon news job. He suggested I call Bob, who in turn asked me to fly in for a chat. Within a few days, I was sitting in his office, considering a job offer but leaning towards not taking it. That's when Bob suggested we go chat with Paul Ski, the wunderkind who had managed CJCH to the top of the Halifax ratings, with the likes of Brian Phillips, Dave Wright, Randy Dewell, and Gregg Lee burning up the airwaves around the clock. Paul, the inveterate workaholic, was in his office on this particular Saturday afternoon and had a few minutes to see me.

Paul was baffled about why I was balking at an opportunity to move to Halifax, which was a bigger market, and to CJCH which was, he proudly pointed out, part of the mighty CHUM group. This was something I was already keenly aware of; Derek Chase, a radio veteran who had returned to CFBC after stints in Ottawa and Windsor/Detroit, had been singing CHUM's praises to me for several years. He was particularly fond of the wit and writing of CHUM commentator Dick Smyth, whose editorials were carried daily on a circuit we could monitor in the CFBC newsroom. On a clear night, a young radiophile could also tune in 1050-CHUM Toronto—and I frequently did. So when Paul Ski spoke about unspecified future opportunities within the group, he piqued my interest. I returned to Saint John the next day, inclined to make the move to Halifax.

"It's a class organization, kid," he counseled in typical Mark Lee fashion. Mark knew of Paul and had nothing but respect for the CHUM organization, particularly Fred Sherratt, for whom he had once worked. Mark didn't tell me to take the job but he knew he couldn't stop me from going as he had a few months earlier. On my last day at CFBC, Mark called me into his office.

"Just one request before you go, kid. Whatever you do in Halifax, promise me you won't touch Mennier. We've got plans for him here in Saint John." It was a promise I had every intention of keeping. But as fate would have it, it wouldn't be up to me.

Surprising Decisions

IT TURNED OUT MY ARRIVAL AT CJCH IN MAY 1980 was part of a wave of change at the radio station. Within weeks, Bob Bishop announced he was leaving for CBC Radio in Toronto. Chuck Bridges, who was running the news department at sister station C100 FM, was tapped to run the combined newsroom. Appointed news supervisor, essentially I was Chuck's assistant, with particular responsibility for the CJCH side of things. One of my first duties was to begin searching for a night news editor to replace Joe Snider, who had opted to move on. Chuck was aware of a possible replacement, a young up-and-comer in New Brunswick named Paul Mennier—and hadn't I worked with him? After admitting that I knew him well, Chuck asked me to place the call, inviting Paul to come to Halifax for an interview. I was torn between my promise to Mark Lee and my obligation to Chuck, but in the end made my decision and hoped that Mark would understand. I called Paul; he came to Halifax and accepted the job. Then I called Mark. Like the professional I knew he was, Mark listened to my explanation, said he appreciated the call, and concluded by saying he didn't consider what I had done

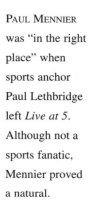

PAUL MENNIER was "in the right place" when sports anchor Paul Lethbridge left *Live at 5*. Although not a sports fanatic, Mennier proved a natural.

a promise broken. More than twenty years later, Mark Lee remains extremely proud of the role he played in launching the broadcasting careers of a couple of kids from Saint John. He also remains a good friend.

Paul was only seventeen years old when he signed on as evening news editor on CJ radio in 1981. He was so young, in fact, his father had to sign his first contract! The rest, as they say, is history.

"If you want to find yourself in the right place at the right time, start by putting yourself in the right place." That's about the only advice I ever offer aspiring broadcasters hungry to land a first job in a fiercely competitive business. For some, being in the right place requires volunteering in a newsroom (or any workplace) and waiting to be noticed. For others, it means taking a job in a less-than-ideal place (usually a small town and a long way from home) just to get on the air. And on the air anywhere is "the right place" for people who aspire to bigger stations or bigger markets.

When the job anchoring the sports on *Live at 5* became available, Paul Mennier was in the right place at the right time. After a couple of years "playing radio" in Halifax, Paul had decided to return to Saint John to pursue a bachelor's degree at the University of New Brunswick. At the time, I found it hard to discourage the idea inasmuch as Paul was doing exactly what I had promised my own parents I would do: return to school after a year in broadcasting. (I'm now in the twenty-fourth year of my "year off.") Besides, Paul was worried that radio might not be much of a career. But Paul didn't have much of a university career, either. After a semester, he was itching to get back on the air and CJCH was glad to have him back. He was an invaluable, all-purpose announcer and a competent newsman. He could even deliver a rapid-fire sportscast with enthusiasm, something many solid newsreaders have trouble with.

Before long, ATV's Paul Lethbridge suggested Paul Mennier make the move to TV as a sportscaster. The station needed someone to anchor sports on *The ATV Sunday Evening News* and *The ATV Late Evening News*. When Lethbridge decided to leave *Live at 5* in late 1983, Paul Mennier was in the right place at the right time: he landed the job.

In some ways, Mennier was a surprising choice to replace Lethbridge on *Live at 5*. For starters, and by his own admission, he didn't know much about sports. A few years in radio had equipped him with enough knowledge to get by: he knew the names of teams and the pre-eminent players in each sport (he adamantly denies ever calling golfer Chi- Chi Rodriguez "Chye-chye Rodragueeze," although I swear I remember hearing it), but he didn't live and breathe sports the way some sportscasters do. He was also young—about twenty-one—but looked as young as sixteen. Harris Sullivan, who emerged as an early Paul Mennier fan, knew instinctively that these shortcomings would be overcome by skill, style, and enthusiasm. He also pegged Paul as a quick study. Harris was right on all counts (and not for the first or last time; he developed a reputation as an uncanny judge of talent), perhaps in part because he saw in Paul Mennier things that reminded him of his younger self. Paul also got plenty of guidance and support from another old sportscaster, Dave Wright, who instantly recognized Mennier's burgeoning talent for sports. In fact, it is Dave who deserves the credit for dreaming up the idea for something that became Paul's trademark and something he delivered better than just about anyone else: "Plays of the Week."

With his love of sports and knowledge of television production, Dave was already a fan of Werner Wolf, who was producing a sports plays "highlights" package on CBS television. Dave even ran the Wolf plays on *Live at 5*, in the early days. But in Paul he saw a young man with the ability (and work ethic) to take a good idea and make it better. He encouraged Paul to utilize all of ATV's considerable news sources, to assemble the wackiest and most amazing sports moments he could find, and put them in a two-and-a-half-minute package. What would set Paul's plays apart were the local, regional, and national excerpts (particularly hockey) that were not available or of interest to Werner Wolf. Paul's writing, punchy and clever, combined with his quick and resonant delivery made for a unique play-by-play commentary. His occasional use of non-sporting events like building implosions and fan antics made the package outrageous and unpredictable, and it was an instant hit. Paul was also a master of the double entendre. Nobody loved Paul's clever quips more than Dave, who could usually be heard cackling or cheering in the background during what I later dubbed "the Friday funnies." A few years later, I prevailed on Paul to add "Plays of the Weekend" to the *Live at 5* lineup, giving viewers a double dose of what had become (and remains) one of our most popular features. Each year, Paul put together "Plays of the Year," and in 1992 a special "reel" marked *Live at 5's* first ten years on the air.

In the fall of 1997, after more than twelve years at ATV, Paul Mennier packed hundreds of "plays" scripts into a trunk and headed for Vancouver. He placed the franchise in the capable hands of another whiz kid, Paul Hollingsworth, son of the veteran newspaperman and sometime Nova Scotia politico Al. For the twentieth anniversary of *Live at 5,* perhaps the Pauls should team up for the "plays of the millennium."

PAUL HOLLINGSWORTH worked his way into an on-air job after volunteering behind the scenes in the ATV newsroom.

Two other nationally familiar faces handled sports in the early days of *Live at 5*. Steve Jacobs is one of the weather presenters on CTV flagship station CFTO in Toronto. He's also seen regularly on *CTV Newsnet* and is the voice of the popular "Lifeline" feature, which runs on *The ATV Evening News* and on many other CTV affiliates.

Colleen Jones was another Harris Sullivan discovery— Colleen the television broadcaster, that is! She was already a Canadian curling champion in the early eighties when Harris lured her away from CJCH radio, which had given the young Colleen her first shot at sportscasting. Colleen proved an able reader, but where she really shone was in live situations, which is where she now finds herself virtually every morning on

Colleen Jones was already a curling
star and a Canadian champion when
she was discovered for television by
Harris Sullivan.

another channel. Over the years, ATV has given many other
broadcasters early breaks in TV. Among them, CKY-Winnipeg's
Janet Stewart, CBC TV's Keith Boag, CNN's Colleen
MacEdwards, and, coincidentally, all three anchors of the
Halifax-based supper-hour newscasts: CBC's Linda Kelly,
Global's Allan Rowe, and...me! ATV's Steve Murphy.

A Matter of Opinion

IN HINDSIGHT, IT WAS ALMOST TOO GOOD TO BE TRUE. For most of the 1980s, I was paid to express my opinions, on radio by day and on television by night. There is nothing quite like the freedom of being allowed to say almost anything you want, about any subject you want, within certain reasonable (legal) limits.

The Hotline provided the greatest freedom of all, and in some respects, the greatest challenge. With a different topic everyday and twice weekly "listeners' choice" programmes, we tackled virtually any subject under the sun. Maintaining a reasonably informed opinion about everything from Soviet politics to Spryfield traffic problems required a great deal of reading and reliable research. Over the years, I was fortunate to have several extremely good producers: Dawn Veinotte, Karen Shewbridge, my former wife Noreen Nunn, and Dianne Coish. Besides preparing invaluable files on the hot topics of the day, each producer was also well versed on who to call to get more information on a certain topic or to get a problem solved. A hot topic on the phone-in show one morning was frequently the subject for a radio commentary the next. Sometimes the subject was repeated on *Live at 5,* but more often than not the television pieces were original and designed for a regional audience. Radio topics were usually Halifax focused.

When Dick Prat first approached me late in summer of 1982 about appearing as a commentator on the *Live at 5* programme, the idea was that I would tackle Maritime topics, leaving national subjects to Toronto-based Dick Smyth, whose brilliant writing and magnificent delivery I had always admired. And that's pretty well the way it went. For the next four years, I was on TV two or three nights a week, commenting on everything from Trivial Pursuit to the accidental sinking of a fishing boat by the Canadian Navy. The topics were usually of my own choosing, although from time to time Dick, Harris, or ATV assignment editors Dave Harrigan or John Soosaar would suggest a topic. Harris or John also offered thoughts on the style and structure of the piece, always leaving the point of view to me. Never once in five years did any management person at ATV or CJCH radio tell me what position to take on an issue, and only rarely was a piece vetoed for legal reasons.

As is often the case in journalism, the commentaries were usually improved in the editing process. In fact, the best line in one of my editorials came from John Soosaar. The piece was about fisherman Walter Theriault, whose twenty-fifth wedding anniversary celebration was rudely interrupted by the Navy sinking his boat! Declared a hazard to navigation, the boat was torpedoed. Nobody was exactly sure who had given the order to sink the vessel, and, after the fact, no one in Maritime Command was willing to take the credit. Theriault's misfortune prompted me to write a "can you believe it?" commentary, which John read and approved. Handing the copy back to me, John quipped, "Well, at least we now know the Canadian Navy is capable of sinking an unmanned, unarmed ship!" That deliciously sarcastic comment became the last line of my piece about the Theriault case, a commentary which won an Atlantic Journalism Award.

The commentaries provoked a substantial reaction from viewers of this new *Live at 5*. We were in fact soliciting responses and broadcasting them every so often. Occasionally, Harris sent out a camera to videotape a viewer reading a particularly

A MAGAZINE AD for Steve Murphy's early eighties morning radio show. He editorialized on *Live at 5* in the afternoons.

"colourful" response, which usually rebutted a particularly controversial editorial. I unleashed a verbal firestorm in 1983 by criticizing Boy George, the sexually ambivalent lead singer of the British pop group Culture Club. His appearance on the cover of *Newsweek* magazine prompted me to wonder out loud about what sort of an influence he was on children. Music television was in its infancy, and Culture Club was big—on television and on radio. The avalanche of mail I received reflected that fact. Some respondents likened my anti-George sentiments to the mid-fifties criticism of a young man from Tupelo, Mississippi, whose wild hip gyrations struck some people as just a little too provocative. Hindsight has judged Boy George no Elvis Presley, but he didn't exactly corrupt an entire generation of children.

The *Live at 5* commentaries weren't just about generating controversy. Designed to lead public opinion, they did so no

STEERING THE SHIP. Executive Producer Harris Sullivan (centre) with Paul Mennier (left) and Regional Assignment Editor John Soosaar. Their cluttered work space was called "the bridge."

more than during the tumultuous weeks following the discovery of marijuana in Richard Hatfield's luggage. The eccentric New Brunswick premier was hosting the queen when drugs were discovered in his personal baggage as it was inspected before being loaded onto an aircraft in Fredericton. He immediately and adamantly denied that the drugs belonged to him; he was later acquitted on criminal charges arising from the drug discovery. When Hatfield was later accused of supplying hard drugs to a group of underage boys in his Fredericton home, we aired a commentary calling on Hatfield to resign, "if the accusations were true." They were never proven and Hatfield remained premier until the Progressive Conservatives suffered the worst defeat in New Brunswick political history. The drug allegations were widely seen as the last straw for thousands of New Brunswickers, including many "dyed in the wool" Tories.

Come election day, October 13, 1987, New Brunswickers voted en masse for the Liberals under a young Miramichi lawyer, Frank McKenna. The final score: Liberals 58, Tories 0. In an ATV commentary, I later praised Hatfield for staying to take his medicine rather than quit politics. Others were not so kind,

HALIFAX ASSIGNMENT EDITOR David Harrigan (left) reviews news copy with Reporter Robert Rankin in the mid-eighties.

blaming Hatfield's considerable ego for a wipeout that might have been averted under a different leader.

Something I said in a *Live at 5* commentary really aggravated newspaper publisher David Bentley and he's never gotten over it. During the 1983 royal visit of Prince Charles and Princess Diana, Bentley and his wife Diana were invited to a reception aboard the royal yacht *Britannia*. It was a strictly off-the-record affair, during which all of the comments of the prince and princess were private and not for publication. Every other media person who attended the event understood and accepted that condition. The Bentleys apparently did not. The next morning *The Daily News* published a story under Diana Bentley's byline which included direct quotations from the young princess. It was a stunt fit for the scandal sheets of London's Fleet Street, where David Bentley had polished his craft. On television that night, I criticized the article as an outrageous breach of protocol by "an upstart Halifax newspaper." Later, on radio, I suggested that readers who were offended by the violation of royal privacy might stop buying the paper and even boycott those who advertised in it. While he has never spoken with me about this—or anything else—I am reliably informed that my comments of almost twenty years ago were the inspiration for the anonymous, unrelenting, and malicious personal attacks directed at me and at *Live at 5* for the dozen or so years Bentley published his little supermarket magazine. It has always struck me as strange, not to mention hypocritical, that a journalist whose motto was to be "frank by nature" about everyone else was so thin-skinned by nature about himself.

My role as commentator provided me with a front-row seat for some of the most fascinating political events of the eighties. I was at Lansdowne Park in Ottawa in 1983 when Brian Mulroney defeated Joe Clark to become leader of the PC party. I stood not twenty feet from Mulroney as he took the stage in triumph. Months later, I covered the meeting in Trenton, Nova Scotia, during which Brian Mulroney was nominated to run as the PC candidate in the riding of Central Nova. Elmer MacKay resigned his long-held seat in parliament to trigger the by-election that would make Mr. Mulroney a member of parliament. It was a love-in during which the pawky Pictounians displayed genuine enthusiasm and affection for the man they sensed would lead the Conservatives out of the political wilderness. There was even greater admiration for Mila Mulroney, who was, on that evening and on every other occasion at which I was present, the picture of dignity and grace, a thoroughly charming person who later did an outstanding job as wife of the prime minister.

Several months later, I found myself back inside a steamy Ottawa Civic Centre for the coronation of John Turner as leader of the Liberal Party and erstwhile prime minister of Canada. "Hello John, Bye Bye Mulroney," the buttons proclaimed. The meaning was clear: Turner can beat Mulroney. But the message was wrong. Several weeks later, Turner called an election and proceeded to stumble his way through a summer campaign that handed the PCs their first majority government since John Diefenbaker. Later, as host of *Live at 5,* I would interview both Mulroney and Turner at length; I found each man to be very much unlike the men they appeared to be.

The Working Newsroom

IT WASN'T LONG BEFORE Dick Prat decided his new evening news programme needed a new home. *Live at 5* was being staged in ATV's Halifax newsroom, which had been built in a TV studio several years earlier. Dick Prat's office, also in the newsroom, was roughly in the middle of the set; the glass door of his office could sometimes be heard slamming—both by accident and by design. On such a set there was little privacy for Prat and his guests, who were often employees being dealt with by their boss.

Back in the days before political correctness and common sense had taken hold, the "working newsroom" was also a "smoking newsroom." It was not uncommon to see reporters and producers smoking cigarettes in the background of *The ATV Evening News*, butting them in ashtrays the size of pizza pans. Bruce Graham was known to keep one going on a shelf under the anchor desk…during the newscast! If you watch carefully on the old tapes or "air checks" from the period, you can actually see smoke encircling Bruce's head.

ATV News was awarded a citation from the Lung Association when Dick, a strident but not militant non-smoker, prohibited cigarette smoking in the newsroom, which was, after all, also

an on-air studio. For several years thereafter, the nicotine addict-
ed, myself included, puffed away in a short hallway that led
from the shipping and receiving dock to the newsroom. An ash-
tray to the immediate left of the doorway leading to the newsroom was constantly overflowing with disgusting cigarette
butts. This state of affairs continued until the Mulroney
government outlawed smoking in all federally-regulated build-
ings, including ATV and every other radio and television station
in the land.

Smoking wasn't the only problem in the old ATV newsroom.
Beyond the obvious difficulty of having the news director's
office in the middle of newsroom, the place had a drab, sort of
low-tech look about it. It didn't send the right message to ATV's
viewers. Dick Prat and Harris Sullivan decided it needed to be
replaced with something flashier. Wrestling the money from
Fred Sherratt and Joe Irvine was the easy part. After getting the
go-ahead, Prat and Sullivan realized they would need a place to
stage the news while the newsroom was torn apart and rebuilt.
There was a second studio at ATV (the one where The Beast and
Killer Karl Krupp had once wrestled on Atlantic Grand Prix
Wrestling) where commercials were made, but it was otherwise
empty. Worried the news programmes would have a totally different look if they were broadcast from a set in 'Studio A'—in
television, "totally different" is exactly what viewers don't
want—Dick and Harris came up with a simple but brilliant solution: move the old newsroom into the second studio while extensive renovations were carried out for the new newsroom. And
that's exactly what they did. One weekend in the summer of
1985, the walls, fixtures, desks, and typewriters were moved,
piece-by-piece, through the double doors separating the two studios. When *Live at 5* viewers turned on their TV sets Monday
night, they had no idea that what they were seeing was an illusion—a newsroom "shell" dropped into a television studio. So
convincing was the recreation that even the landlord didn't
know the difference.

Allan Waters, owner of the station, was paying one of his rare
visits to ATV when he encountered Ian Morrison in a cluttered

ANCHOR BRUCE GRAHAM in ATV's original "low-tech" working newsroom.

hallway. Waters was curious about all the drop sheets and saw-dust and wondered what was going on. Ian, by then senior pro-ducer of news for ASN (which was still staged at the opposite end of the ATV News studio), explained that the newsroom was being rebuilt. The proprietor was perplexed. Hadn't he seen the newsroom on the air, just last night? A quick tour explained it all to the amazement and amusement of the man who was ultimately paying for it.

The at-home viewers may have been totally unaware of this harmless deception but they couldn't help but notice what hap-pened next. Susan Dunn had been hosting the weather on ATV News for several years when she announced she was leaving the station. The decision created a major void in the on-air line-up. Susan had developed a loyal following for her forecasts and environmental reports after being brought in to replace the enor-mously popular Marcia Andrews, who had chosen to pursue other interests in Vancouver in 1980. Harris Sullivan knew replacing Susan would not be easy, possibly even risky. The key players on *Live at 5* had developed a certain "chemistry," so he needed to find someone who would fit into the family. He had

SUSAN DUNN, working with the first weather computer in Canadian television. Her decision to leave *Live at 5* punched a hole in the on-air lineup.

been speaking on and off with a young Cape Breton radio reporter who really wanted a career in television. She had a bit of experience, a lot of confidence, and most importantly a huge amount of personality. Harris believed she could step into Susan's role as weather presenter, and that she might even have what it takes to become a features reporter and, ultimately, a co-host. Prat, who had enormous respect for Sullivan's ability to judge talent, accepted the recommendation to hire Laura Lee Langley.

Laura Lee was the first person hired to work on *Live at 5* whose only knowledge of the programme had come from watching it. Paul Mennier and I were insiders who had worked on the radio side of the TV building. Dave and Debi had been with ATV for years. Laura Lee was clearly star struck when she turned up for her first day of work in the makeshift studio where, fortunately for her, smoking had not yet been banned. Perched sheepishly at the weather desk, she sat puffing her nerves away when I walked over and introduced myself. She knew me as the commentator on *Live at 5,* which she quickly told me was must-see TV in the Sydney home of Parker and Faye Langley. I was later

CAPE BRETON RADIO PERSONALITY Laura Lee Langley—the first person hired to host *Live at 5* whose only knowledge of the programme had come just from watching it!

to learn that was no exaggeration. Not only were the Langleys tremendous fans and supporters of the show (before and after their first-born was part of it), they were also extremely warm and generous people who opened their house to the *Live at 5* crew anytime we were in the neighbourhood. Faye and Parker regularly showed up when we broadcasted from the island, usually with a small and enthusiastic group of friends who cheered us on. In this way, the Langleys reminded me of my own parents, who have always come out to the live shows. And there were to be plenty of live shows for Laura Lee and me, although we had no way of knowing that when we first shook hands on that day in the summer of '85.

Harris had done it again. His instincts about Laura Lee Langley had been right on the money. She turned out to be "God-gifted good" at live television and a natural at telling feature stories. Part of the reason she worked out so well is that she had a great deal of performing experience—not on television, there she was a rookie—but on stage as a dancer. She was also a veteran of several pageants, where she had learned poise and self-confidence. Being a Maritime local didn't hurt either.

She knew the area and the people and had great affection for both, and it showed. Viewers took to the young Cape Bretoner instantly and everyone at the station liked her too. Her role on *Live at 5* began to expand almost immediately and she was already a featured player on the show when the phone rang at my house on a sweltering July day with the news about Dave.

Dick Prat had approached me about becoming Dave Wright's permanent fill-in on *Live at 5* several months before Dave announced he was leaving the station. I was scheduled to co-host the programme during Dave's July 1986 vacation. His departure accelerated that by a couple of weeks but it led to speculation that I was the frontrunner to succeed Dave as host of *Live at 5*. The final decision, in fact, had not been made yet, nor would it be for at least a couple of months. Harris Sullivan says Dick Prat had more than a hundred applications for the job and several candidates who deserved and received serious consideration. In "Who will follow Dave?" Cliff Boutilier of the Halifax *Daily News* speculated about who might step into the position.

Boutilier named *ATV Evening News* anchor Bruce Graham, *Atlantic Pulse* anchor Ron Kronstein, and "talk show host"

STEVE MURPHY succeeds
Dave Wright as *Live at 5* host,
October 1986.

Steve Murphy as three candidates, with late news anchor Bill McKay a likely fourth. For his part, Harris Sullivan would only say, "there's no question the new man will have very large shoes to fill...Dave was a tremendous idea man." That was an understatement. Dave was not only involved in deciding which local stories ran on *Live at 5*, he also selected and decided the order for all of the entertainment, medical, and other feature items. These television-producing skills were totally foreign to me when I started substituting for Dave. And the learning curve would have been considerably steeper were it not for the generous assistance of the established production team.

Production assistant Dawn Veinotte and videotape editor Art Steeves had worked with Dave so long they could practically read his mind. Director Ken Publicover quickly schooled the rookie in the fine art of timing a television programme. The decision to give the job to me was never formally announced, but after four months as the temporary guy, and with the strong support of Harris Sullivan, I was made permanent in October 1986. My two-year contract called for me to continue with *The Hotline* show and *The Noon Report* on radio, which, together with hosting *Live at 5* in the afternoon, made for long days, days that became even longer when Dick, Harris, and Ian decided ATV should "celebrate the Maritimes."

Something to Celebrate

THE IDEA FOR "CELEBRATE THE MARITIMES" came from Jacques deSuze, who borrowed it shamelessly (as he was paid to do) from a station in Phoenix, Arizona. The idea sounded simple enough: take *Live at 5* out of the studio environment into communities across the Maritimes, for fairs and festivals or just for the fun of it. Dave Wright had done something similar at the Annapolis Valley Apple Blossom Festival and various church suppers, and, of course, in London and Poland. But those shows had been pre-recorded, edited, and played back to look live. The plan this time was to really go live—via satellite—from places where live television had never been done before. And not just once or once a week, but twice a week every week for the entire summer of 1987! And that, it turned out, was just the beginning.

Dick Prat had always dreamed of having a news helicopter, and in June 1987 it looked like his dream had finally come true. The ATV News chopper, covered with colourful ATV logos, actually belonged to Cougar Helicopters, a charter company operating out of the heli-pad on the Halifax waterfront. Dick had convinced Cougar to be part of "Celebrate the Maritimes." He also prevailed on a Truro firm to furnish a twenty-eight-foot

HITTING THE ROAD, 1986. *Live at 5* rolls out on a summer-long mission to "celebrate the Maritimes."

Empress motor-home to be used as a mobile newsroom and editing suite by day and crew quarters (and party headquarters) by night. Add a couple of ATV's commodious Crown Victoria wagons, a large cube van, the station's "mini mobile" production vehicle, and a futuristic satellite uplink truck, all splashed with ATV logos, and you had a pretty impressive caravan—more like a parade—with a mission to "celebrate the Maritimes."

The celebrating began on July 1, 1987, with an ambitious three-city production to mark Canada's 120th birthday and premiere what was to be a summer of live broadcasts on *Live at 5*. Laura Lee Langley was dispatched to the cradle of Confederation to cover events in Charlottetown. ATV New Brunswick news director Pat Ryan was stationed on the Green along the St. John River in Fredericton, and I was set up to go live from Grand Parade in Halifax. We had a handful of video-taped stories ready but most of the show was to be live, with special guests in each city and a lot of spontaneous bi-play with the throngs of people expected at each location. This three-province extravaganza was to set the tone for the "Celebrate the Maritimes" series, which would fan out across Nova Scotia,

CELEBRATE VIA
SATELLITE!
The satellite and
production trucks
used to "beam"
fairs and festivals
into Maritime
living rooms.

New Brunswick, and PEI. So you can well imagine how everyone felt when the show was pre-empted; knocked off the air by
the Blue Jays-Expos baseball game, which at five o'clock on
Canada Day had gone into extra innings!

We were all told to stand by, on the understanding we would
go on the air as soon as Don Chevrier and Fergie Olver signed
off. So "stand by" we did, literally hovering around a nine-inch
black-and-white television set, watching in rapt anticipation of
the last pitch that would bring us up to plate. Six o'clock came,
the end of the game didn't. Then six-thirty and seven o'clock.
Finally, sometime after 7:15, the tie was broken, and CTV sent
word down the line that local programming could be resumed
at 7:30. At that stage, Dick Prat and programming czar Joe
Irvine could easily have decided to send us all home, shaving a
few dollars off the quickly mounting overtime bill (by now,
some of the technicians were earning well into double time on
a statutory holiday). They opted instead, in the best show business tradition, to let the show go on. Bruce Graham's *ATV
Evening News* at six would air at 7:30, followed by *Live at 5* at
eight o'clock. It was during Bruce's newscast that it suddenly

dawned on us that we had a problem. The huge crowds that earlier had squeezed in around our live locations had all gone home
for supper! Pat Ryan was left standing pretty much by himself
"on the Green" and I was in the same boat in the Grand Parade.
And that wasn't all. Faced with a flight deadline she couldn't
change, Laura Lee had been forced to pre-record her segments
of the show, meaning we wouldn't be able to eat up time chit-
chatting on the air, as we usually did. A quick assessment of our
situation concluded we had no more than twenty-five minutes
worth of content (plus commercials) to fill a one-hour programme, which by now had been dubbed "The *Live at 5* Prime
Time Special."

I had a knot in my stomach as the "Celebrate the Maritimes"
theme music and opening animation went to air for the first time.
Director Donnie Verge, a seasoned veteran of countless live
broadcasts, had offered me quiet and comforting words of support, while admitting there would have to be some "tap dancing" (filling up time with adlibs). The show went to air in pretty much the order we had planned, and by 8:30 or so we were
just about out of material. That's when I caught a glimpse of Ian
Morrison marching down George Street (the street that slopes
from the Halifax Metro Centre to the Grand Parade) leading a
parade of characters from the world-renowned Nova Scotia
International Tattoo.

Ian had paid a quick and desperate visit to Colonel Ian Fraser,
the Tattoo producer, who had graciously seconded some of his
performers to appear on our show. Colonel Fraser was undoubtedly moved by the plight of a fellow producer whose live show
was in jeopardy. He was also clever enough to recognize the
value of a prime-time commercial for the Tattoo on the
Maritimes' number one television station.

Fraser's cast of characters lined up for what amounted to an
old style inspection on live TV. I spoke with each about their
role in the Tattoo, their costume, and their hometown. It made
for surprisingly interesting and colourful television and neatly
filled the remaining time in our prime-time special. When it was
over, we all retreated to the motor home, where we heaved a

ON LOCATION in Saint John. Steve Murphy and Laura Lee Langley originate "Celebrate the Maritimes" from Saint John's Festival by the Sea.

sigh of relief and hoisted a jar of cheer. None of the more than sixty "Celebrate the Maritimes" shows that followed seemed as difficult as that first one, although several were also near disasters.

The next day, the show went on the road. An advance team led by Donnie and Ian set out by caravan for Sherbrooke Village, Nova Scotia, the charming and authentic recreation of the nineteenth-century Guysborough County gold-mining town. On the brilliantly sunny morning of July 3, 1987, Laura Lee and I "choppered-in," undoubtedly making quite a scene as our Bell Long Ranger touched down in a field near the village. It was to be the first of many such landings. With ex-airforce pilot Earl MacFarlane at the controls and adventurer Ingo Strackerjan beside him, we zipped across the Maritimes that summer, traveling from as far north as Caraquet, New Brunswick to Louisbourg in the east, south to Bridgewater, west to Point d'Eglise, and twenty stops in between.

Since helicopters fly so much lower than fixed-wing planes, the view of what's below is often much more spectacular. And so it was as Laura Lee and I crisscrossed the Maritimes from

IAN MORRISON. The veteran reporter and producer stage-managed most of the "Celebrate the Maritimes" programmes.

three hundred to one thousand feet. It was during that summer that I first came to appreciate the rugged and breathtaking beauty of the Fundy cliffs, only a few kilometres east of where I had been raised. Likewise for the Cabot Trail, an even rarer spectacle from a few hundred feet; the misty, magical tranquility of Caraquet Bay; the soft pink dusk blending seamlessly with the red-brown mud of Minas Basin at low tide. Every flight was an education in the geography and topography of an area I thought I knew like the back of my hand.

Only once did a helicopter trip strike fear into our hearts. We were headed to the famous Lobster Carnival in Shediac when we encountered fog that had rolled up the Bay of Fundy and was laying in a thick bank just the other side of Truro. Earl and Ingo wisely decided to land the chopper at the former military airfield in Debert and wait for the fog to lift, which it was likely to do as the tide retreated and the sun rose higher in the sky. After we sipped a couple of cups of instant coffee with the fliers at the glider school, the tower at Halifax International Airport, satisfied that the fog had cleared, gave permission for the chopper to take off. The decision proved a bit premature. Just min-

TAKE ME OUT TO THE FAIR!
Steve and Laura Lee on the
midway at The Big Ex in
Bridgewater, Nova Scotia,
1987.

utes out of the Debert field, we were again shrouded in fog, with
Earl and Ingo looking for a highway to follow. They suggested
Laura Lee and I keep an eye on the treetops below—the ones
we could see—and inform them immediately if we were getting
too close. Put another way, they wanted to know when the trees
started rising up the slope of Folly Mountain, which lay ahead,
although they couldn't see exactly where. Sure enough, the trees
started getting closer. Earl put the chopper into a fairly steep
climb and we cleared the summit of Folly with only metres to
spare. With clear skies on the other side, we carried on to
Shediac, where later that day thunderstorms gave way to a
sticky and sunny afternoon and a successful show.

There were no more "close calls" that summer, although Ian
chose not to tell Laura Lee and me about a helicopter crash near
Halifax airport the afternoon we flew home from the Irish
Festival on the Miramichi, which is just as well.

The summer of 1987 stands out as one of the most enjoyable
and memorable of my working life. We visited historic sights,
feasted on seafood, haggis, and rappie pie, were feted at fairs
and festivals; most importantly, we met thousands of *Live at 5*

"WHEN IN NEW GLASGOW...."
Irishman dons Scottish attire at The
Festival of the Tartans in New
Glasgow, Nova Scotia.

viewers. It was a lot of work, especially for our camerapeople, editors, floor directors, engineers, satellite technicians, and producers...but it was a lot of fun. It was also a big hit. Viewer response was immediate and enthusiastic. By the spring of 1988, we were receiving dozens of invitations from communities, large and small, to "Celebrate the Maritimes" at their fair or festival, invitations we were pleased to accept.

Grey Clouds

"CELEBRATE" WAS RENEWED FOR A SECOND SEASON, with some changes. The helicopter was replaced with an amphibious plane, operated by Air Integra, a charter company that had fearless Ingo Strackerjan as one of its principals. The Empress gave way to a slightly larger motor home called the Bounder. The production schedule was only slightly less ambitious, calling for at least one live show every week, with two some weeks. Laura Lee and I flew mostly with Air Integra, landing on rivers, bays, and harbours from Saint John to Louisbourg.

The first show in the summer of '88 was from Bridgetown, Nova Scotia, which just happened to be the hometown of Dick Prat. The occasion was American Visitors Appreciation Day. It was a sunny and warm July 4 right up until five o'clock, when the sky opened. The crew scrambled into yellow rain suits; Laura Lee and I dodged puddles under huge umbrellas. No one could understand where the storm had come from—it hadn't been forecast and there hadn't been a cloud in the sky up until minutes before show time. Our queries were answered during Laura Lee's five-thirty weather forecast, when the satellite picture, inserted by the Halifax control room direct from the weather computer, revealed one and only one dark grey blotch over the south-west Annapolis Valley…directly over the boss's hometown. The rainstorm lasted exactly forty-five minutes; by the time the show signed off, the sun was shining. You can well imagine the caustic quips about Dick "having a grey cloud over his head" that ensued. Thereafter, anytime he showed up on a location we joked about the chance of rain. But in truth we were always well prepared for inclement weather, having learned a painful and embarrassing lesson two years earlier on a day when we weren't prepared.

It was the day John Hughes came home from a solo sail around the world. He didn't do it in record time but he did it in a jury-rigged sailboat, the main sail having been lost as he rounded South America. It was quite an accomplishment, something people in his home port of Halifax were very proud of and planned to celebrate. To Dick Prat, a sailor, it sounded like good TV. Dick had visions of a flotilla of boats, large and small, surrounding John on his triumphant sail up Halifax Harbour to the Dartmouth Yacht Club. He laid out plans for an expansive special, with eight cameras on the ground, in the air, and even on John Hughes's boat. Dick wanted to let ATV viewers see and hear the returning hero in the final minutes of his global odyssey. It should have been great television, it would have been great television, were it not for the fog and the rain.

"Weather office says it's a shower," pronounced Jim Hill as I arrived at the yacht club wearing my best blue blazer, white shirt, and burgundy tie. Paul Mennier and I had chosen to adopt "the yacht club look" for our afternoon co-hosting the Hughes homecoming. Ninety minutes before air, a light rain was falling, but we were assured it was nothing to worry about. An hour later, with raindrops the size of gumdrops pounding down on our van, Paul, reporter Heather Proudfoot, Jim Hill, and I tried to have a production meeting, but we couldn't hear ourselves over what sounded like a drum solo on the roof. At that point, someone decided to break out the yellow rain suits. With fifteen minutes until the start of our live show, Paul and I hop-scotched around the large puddles that were forming, trying to get to the anchor position, a desk perched perilously on a web of electrical cables. Pointing out the very shock hazard that Paul and I had both been thinking about, floor director John "Soupy" Campbell counseled caution as we took our seats. We didn't get "fried," but unfortunately our television monitors did. They were recessed into the desk, so that they were unseen by the viewers but visible to us. Each one sizzled and popped as its protective "garbage bag" was removed. The driving rain had the same effect on our cameras, although not as quickly. The gear on John's boat, which performed perfectly in rehearsals, didn't work at all during the show, the rain zapped the microwave in the helicopter, so there never were any aerials shots, and the fog which had rolled in made it virtually impossible to see anything on the harbour. Heather Proudfoot, who was supposed to be our roving reporter, ended up attached to a camera with a cable so short she couldn't rove beyond a few metres. The final indignity came when John himself was hustled past our live location without stopping for the promised interview. "Too wet," somebody mumbled. As the last of our eight cameras flickered to black, our television extravaganza effectively reduced to a radio show, Paul and I huddled around a "peanut" (a tiny clip-on microphone) and signed off, voicing over a still shot of an ATV sign.

When it was finally and mercifully over, Dick Prat took Jim Hill, Paul, and myself to the refreshment tent, where he stoically purchased and we each quickly consumed about four fingers of scotch. I remember being cold and angry, the scotch helping with the former. Later, at home on Robie Street, I threw away my once crisp white shirt, sullied as it was with a burgundy tie-shaped stain. Back at the station, they couldn't throw away the waterlogged cameras and other equipment, which took hundreds of hours and tens of thousands of dollars to dry out and repair.

The silver lining behind this particular grey cloud was that following a tempestuous confrontation with Donnie Verge, station manager Marven Nathanson took immediate steps to make sure such a disaster never happened again. He authorized the

purchase of protective coverings for the cameras and a large tent
for the people who stand in front of them. That tent is still known
as the "JH Memorial Tent." At ATV it was and still is considered bad luck to invoke the name of "John Hughes." Mind you,
were it not for him we might not have had the equipment that
kept us dry and on the air during subsequent programmes,
including one in Bridgewater where he showed up as parade
marshall...and it rained!

"Celebrate the Maritimes" had a tremendous impact on the
people who watched the show and the people who worked on
it. For many ATV viewers, particularly those who lived in small
towns, it was a rare opportunity to see how television was made
and to meet the people they watched everyday. Laura Lee and I
spent a great deal of time signing autographs and doing interviews for local radio stations and newspapers. Our technical
staff also turned heads, traveling as they did in an impressive
convoy of brightly logoed vehicles. Given the amount of driving involved in producing such a programme, the Halifax-based
technicians and production team were on the road virtually all
summer. Not surprisingly, they became a tight-knit unit. They
also got to know and work with some of the very talented people from ATV's seven locations around the region.

When "Celebrate the Maritimes" rolled into the Moncton
area, veteran cameramen Al Henry (a dead ringer for TV's Phil
Donahue), Gerry White, and Paul MacEachern, and technician
Larry Wartman were usually called on to join the production
staff. Saint John area shows often relied on the creative and technical talents of cameramen Brian Chisholm, Murray Titus (both
schoolmates of mine at Saint John High), and Mike Burchill. In
Fredericton, Pat Richard and Shawn DeLong got the call. In
Sydney, it was Darryl Reeves, Bruce Hennessey, and Gary
Mansfield. Trainor Donovan was always there as our audio
operator. One of the benefits of the project was that it made
friends out of colleagues, many of whom had previously never
even met. Laura Lee and I became good friends as well. We were
all very proud of the "Celebrate the Maritimes" series, the quality of the work, and the response from the public. Back at the

station, things were not as rosy. By mid-July 1988, morale problems and discontent conspired with opportunity to create the greatest crisis in ATV's history.

The seeds of opportunity had been planted a year and a half earlier, when the Canadian Radio, Television and Telecommunications Commission (CRTC) decided the Maritimes should have another independent television service. On January 22, 1987, over the strong objection of already established broadcasters (including ATV, which believed there wasn't enough advertising money to support another station), New Brunswick Broadcasting Company Limited was granted a license to operate stations in Halifax and Saint John as Maritime Independent Television (MITV). As part of the deal, the Irving family agreed to sell the province-wide transmission facilities of CHSJ-TV to the Canadian Broadcasting Corporation (CBC), thereby finally giving New Brunswick a CBC owned and operated station (CHSJ had been an affiliate). MITV was set to hit the air on September 5, 1988.

The first tremor in an earthquake of change struck ATV just a few days after our July 4 show in Bridgetown. I had flown to Saint John immediately after the broadcast and was visiting with my parents when I got a phone call from Dick Prat. His tone was reminiscent of the call two years earlier when he dropped the bomb about Dave Wright. The news this time was even more shocking. Not only was the esteemed Bruce Graham giving up his anchor chair, he was going "across the harbour." He had been lured by the Irvings personally to run the newsroom and read the evening news at their new station, probably enticed by more money and the promise that he could come off the air at some point to concentrate on documentaries. Upon giving several weeks notice, he had been told his services were no longer required at ATV.

Donnie Verge was the next to go, hired away as operations manager by ex-ATV comptroller Ken Clark, who was managing the new station. A parade of ATV's top technicians followed Donnie, led by chief cameraman Wayne Clark. Several of our "Celebrate the Maritimes" road warriors also decided to leave,

THE CONSUMMATE PRO. Bruce Graham's decision to leave the ATV anchor desk for upstart MITV started an exodus of talented people to the new station in 1988.

CHIEF CAMERAMAN WAYNE CLARK followed Graham across the harbour to MITV.

KELLY RYAN traded her *Live at 5* consumer beat for general news assignments at MITV.

including Mike Trenchard, one of the best "crunch editors" in the business, and cameramen Kendall Nowe and Jamie Munro. Newsroom production assistant Susan Holle jumped at the chance to direct the news at MITV, and we lost several prominent members of the on-air team, including consumer reporter Kelly Ryan, who had been hired from radio after Premier John Buchanan named Debi Forsyth-Smith chair of the Nova Scotia Advisory Council on the Status of Women. ASN anchor Carole McDade went to MITV as a producer, and was joined a few months later by weather forecaster Duane Lowe, who accepted a job hosting a midday talk show. And then, there was Laura Lee. Not relishing her role as "weather girl" and itching to do more serious news reporting on *Live at 5*, Laura Lee couldn't say no when Ken Clark offered her an anchor chair beside Bruce Graham. It was an offer ATV simply could not trump, although Harris, Dick, and Marven Nathanson tried.

The station did manage to hold on to many employees being aggressively courted by MITV, including an up-and-coming

Tired of weather forecasting, Laura Lee Langley opted for a position co-anchoring the news with Bruce Graham at MITV.

young production assistant from Pleasant Point, Nova Scotia. Jocelyn Corkum joined ATV News while studying for her journalism degree at the University of Kings College. She started out in the most entry level position: autocue or teleprompt operator (the person who runs the device that projects scripts over the lens of the camera so anchors don't have to look down while reading), hoping to work up to an on-air job as a sports commentator. But a funny thing happened on the way to the broadcast booth. Ian Morrison, whose duties as senior producer included scheduling the newsroom staff, needed editorial production assistants (PA's), not sports announcers. PA's are critical to television production, but they usually don't get enough credit. They are responsible for the timing of programmes and assist producers and directors in a myriad of other ways before and during live productions. Jocelyn needed the work and, to her own surprise, had already developed considerable interest and ability on the other side of the camera. So, after some hastily arranged training with PA Kelly Smith-Tremblay, Jocelyn rerouted her career path.

Before long, Jocelyn was working on *The ATV Evening News* and other assorted projects, picking up production experience on Paul Mennier's bowling show and field producing many of the "Celebrate the Maritimes" programmes. She was also shadowing director Ken Publicover and displaying considerable skill as a director in her own right. It came as no surprise that Jocelyn was Bruce Graham's first choice for his new newscast at MITV. She considered a good offer but opted to stay at ATV for the same pay MITV offered, and a lot more responsibility. When Ken accepted a job in Florida, Jocelyn was named director of *Live at 5*. Her decision to stay at ATV would ultimately change my life forever—we were married four and a half years later!

Right Time, Right Place

THE "EXODUS OF 88" punched some major holes in ATV's lineup on both sides of the camera, and it might have been the end of the place and its ratings dominance but for three things: Dick Prat's luck, Harris Sullivan's judgement, and MITV's critical mistake.

The "luck," if you can call it that, was in the timing of Dave Wright's decision to forsake the bright lights of the big city for a return to the simpler and less stressful life. Dave had made quite a splash when he first arrived at WNEV-TV in the late summer of 1986, but it wasn't the sort of attention Dave was hoping for. When the station demoted and then fired long-time anchor Tom Ellis, who was well liked although not well watched, some of his fans publicly heaped scorn on "the Canadian" replacing him. Dave's unique style did not go unnoticed and might have propelled Boston's perennial number three station to number one if the people running the place had let Dave be the person they hired. Instead, they took the walking, talking, avuncular Dave and sat him behind a traditional anchor desk. He was quickly dispatched to war-torn Iran, with a Canadian cameraman, where their passports opened doors that were closed and bolted to American journalists. As usual, Dave produced some brilliant stories, which we aired on *Live at 5*. But back in Boston, Dave-at-the desk wasn't bringing in the big ratings; the critics were often brutal and the stress became unbearable. After about a year and half, Dave Wright suffered a massive heart attack while dining with his wife Audrey at a Beantown restaurant. Joking as he was carried out that there was nothing wrong with the food, he was rushed to Massachusetts General Hospital. Donnie Verge got the news from somebody he knew in Boston and word spread quickly throughout the television station. Our concern grew to near panic when we were unable to get any information about his condition. Told there was no patient named David Wright at Mass General, we later learned a "John David Wright" (none of us had known his full name) had been admitted with a heart problem; he was in intensive care in serious condition. The CBC evening newscast *First Edition* broke the news to the general public. We decided not to report anything until we had much more detailed information, which we had by the following evening.

Live at 5 viewers responded to Dave's illness with concern and compassion, sending hundreds of get well cards, flowers, and gifts. Dave and his family were so moved by the outpouring of affection and support from Maritimers that Dave's son Gord appeared on *Live at 5* by telephone from Boston. He spoke emotionally about his father's condition and his family's gratitude. Dave himself agreed to a phone interview with me just before undergoing the quadruple bypass recommended and performed by some of America's best cardiologists. Never one to pass up a good story, Dave allowed cameras in the operating room to capture the surgery on tape, from start to finish. After a brief recovery, Dave produced a truly remarkable series of stories entitled "Straight from the Heart." He was later named "Man of the Year" by the American Heart Foundation.

Dave returned to the WNEV anchor desk, presumably over the objections of his wife and family, but by July 1988 he was ready to give it up for good. The Wrights planned to return to Ontario, where Dave would do some teaching at a broadcasting college and otherwise retire to the tranquility of cottage

country—but then something better came along. The very day
the moving truck arrived in Toronto carrying their furniture
from Boston, Dave received a phone call from Fred Sherratt. It
must have seemed like déjà vu. Sherratt had a vacancy in Halifax
and, once again, Dave was the perfect candidate to fill it. After
some negotiation, Dave Wright was hired to replace Bruce
Graham on *The ATV Evening News*.

Minutes after signing off "Celebrate the Maritimes" from the
Charlottetown Yacht Club, I got the good news in another excited phone call from Dick. Several days later, the Air Integra float
plane was dispatched to pick me up at my former mother-in-
law's cottage on Nova Scotia's St. George's Bay, and return me
to Halifax for a news conference at which we introduced our
once and future colleague. From where I sat, losing Bruce
Graham was a setback, but replacing him with Dave Wright was
just the coup we needed to mitigate the damage.

About a month later, Laura Lee, who had been mulling over
MITV's offer, announced she would quit *Live at 5* to become
Dave's competition. For the second time in two years the show
was looking for a co-host. Fortunately for all of us, we didn't
have to look far. Many people wrongly assume that Nancy
Regan got the job because of her famous surname (Nancy's
father was premier of Nova Scotia and later a federal cabinet
minister).The truth is that, while the name didn't hurt, it wasn't
the main factor in the decision. Nancy turned up as an unpaid
intern in the ATV newsroom shortly after she graduated from
St. Francis Xavier with a degree in arts, in the spring of 1988.
She had sought advice from Harris Sullivan about the best way
to pursue a career in television journalism. While trying to
decide which school to attend and in what discipline, she was
willing to "work" for nothing to learn what she could. That put
Nancy in the right place at the right time when some summer
relief work became available. And her work turned out to be
above average for someone who had neither studied journalism
nor appeared much on television.

Nancy had a great deal of poise, some of which she probably
acquired during her reign as Miss Nova Scotia in 1986, but most

NANCY REGAN had been a newsroom volunteer and part-time reporter when she was named *Live at 5* co-host in the summer of 1988. This is her first ATV publicity shot.

of which she undoubtedly learned from her mother, Carole. Self confident, Nancy had grown up as a politician's daughter, and so was comfortable in the public eye. She was enthusiastically heralded by Harris as "having great potential," which to the cost-conscious Dick Prat also translated into "affordable." When Laura Lee decided to leave, Nancy's was one of the names on a very short list. She was obviously interested in the opportunity to co-host *Live at 5* but was never too keen about working at the weatherboard. For my part, I felt that we shouldn't attempt to replace Laura Lee with another weather personality and argued instead for a meteorologist, someone whose scientific credentials would add a special dimension to our forecasts. As luck would have it, Dick had received a resumé and audition tape from a man who seemed to fit the bill. He was presenting weather and environmental stories on the CBC station in Windsor, Ontario, and was looking for a move. His name was Richard Zurawski.

Forecasting the weather is a thankless job, and forecasting weather on television in Halifax is particularly tough. It's not just that the weather is less predictable here than anywhere else (which Peter Coade says is because of the ocean and its effect) there is also the "Rube" factor. Reuben "Rube" Hornstein's face

RICHARD ZURAWSKI
became ATV's first
meteorologist
in 1988.

was one of the first to flicker onto Halifax television screens
when CBHT signed on in December 1954. He did the weather
forecast on a programme hosted by Max Ferguson, the same
programme on which a young man named Don Tremaine read
the news. Rube was a weather scientist with a knack for explaining the weather and a reputation for getting it right. When I first
saw Rube on CBC's *Gazette* in 1980, he reminded me of Art
Gould and Bayard MacIntyre, the chalk-tossing weathermen on
Saint John's CHSJ-TV, which I watched when I was a kid. They
too had a reputation for uncanny reliability. By the time Rube
"put down the chalk" in the early eighties, he was an icon and
the gold standard against which all future Halifax weather fore-
casters would be judged.

Richard Zurawski was the first "weather scientist" in the
post-Rube era. For most of the eighties, both ATV and CBC had
used weather presenters who had no formal training or experience in meteorology. With a degree in physics and a posting at
Environment Canada's weather service to his credit, Richard
was a meteorologist (although he did not have a diploma in
meteorology and some quarrelled with the use of the title).
There were the inevitable comparisons with the venerable Rube,
whose well-deserved reputation for excellence was further
enhanced by the passage of time. Some viewers were skeptical
but most were impressed, and Richard Zurawski became something of an overnight sensation.

STANDING TALL. The controversial billboard on which Dave Wright and Steve Murphy appear taller than Nancy Regan. She was sitting—they were standing!

All of these personnel changes at the region's most popular television station created quite a buzz in the local news media and even generated some national attention. *Macleans* magazine carried a short story about the billboard campaign launched to promote the new ATV anchor team. At issue was the controversial matter of why Nancy Regan, who was pictured between Dave Wright and Steve Murphy, appeared significantly shorter than the two of us. The suggestion was that it was a deliberate misrepresentation, designed to mask the fact that she was actually the tallest of the three. It was a tantalizing, if specious scandal! The truth is that Dave, Nancy, and I are almost exactly the same height: between five-foot-eight and five-foot-nine. Nancy appeared shorter because she was sitting on a stool, whereas Dave and I were standing. While it's true that on occasion high-tech devices like phonebooks have been used to equalize the height of on-air personalities, such wasn't the case with the billboard campaign.

The first rule of television programming is that consistency is critical. Research suggests and history has proven that viewers don't care to see a lot of major changes on their favourite shows. News programmes in particular are personality driven; viewers develop a sort of rapport with the hosts. And so, in September 1988, with so many familiar faces set to appear on MITV and so many new faces on ATV, there was real concern and curiosity about who would win when the two news teams went head to head. It would have been an interesting contest but it never happened. Instead of challenging *The ATV Evening New*, MITV decided to air its flagship newscast at 7:00 P.M. The

THE NEW ATV TEAM that took on MITV in the fall of 1988.

rationale was that rather than offer viewers a third choice at 6:00 P.M., when both ATV and CBC were already airing news, MITV would give people an alternative. But that decision ignored the obvious fact that Ron Kronstein was anchoring a successful "alternative" newscast on ASN at seven o'clock, and squandered what should have been the new station's greatest advantage: several of ATV's most familiar faces. When people went looking for Bruce and Laura Lee at news time, they were nowhere to be found. MITV had asked people to dramatically change their supper-hour viewing habits…ignoring the first rule of television programming.

A more serious ratings challenge was being mounted by CBC's *First Edition*, where anchor Jim Nunn was well established and hitting his stride just as we were making changes. A very clever news executive named Ron Crocker was running the CBC show, relying on excellent instincts to assign a team of competent reporters. The closest CBC has ever come to regaining its dominance in supper-hour news in Halifax occurred during and shortly after Crocker's tenure. Promoted to Toronto and given responsibility for all of CBC's local newscasts, Crocker has since returned to Atlantic Canada and now presides over the CBC's regional operation.

MITV eventually moved its news to six o'clock but by then it was too late—the people of the Maritimes had stuck with ATV's *Live at 5* and *The ATV Evening News*. We had just won the big game. Next, we were going to Walt Disney World.

We Get Around

ONE OF THE CONDITIONS Dave Wright attached to his return to Halifax was that he not produce *The ATV Evening News*. The station's practice has always been to have the people who anchor the newscasts also put them together. Dave knew how to do that, probably better than anyone else, but argued he didn't want or need the stress of a workday that started at nine o'clock in the morning and ended at six-thirty in the evening. As a concession to his health and his wife, he planned to come into the station around ten-thirty, take lunch everyday, then spend the afternoon polishing his scripts for the newscast. The business of assigning stories after the daily morning meeting, working with reporters, and lining up the show would have to be handled by someone else. The someone else eventually chosen for the job was Mark Campbell.

Mark came highly recommended by the inestimable Max Keeping, long-time anchor and vice-president of news at Ottawa's CJOH-TV. The colourful Newfoundlander had worked in Halifax years earlier, and knew both Dick and Harris. Max had hired Mark for a junior position in his newsroom but knew the young Ottawa native had both the ability and ambition to do considerably more. Producing the news in Halifax sounded like a good opportunity to Mark, who was also excited about the prospect of working with the legendary Dave. The two got along reasonably well, although Dave found it difficult to limit his involvement in the newscast to simply reading it and writing it.

After a few months, Mark was itching to do some traveling and he came up with the idea of taking *Live at 5* to Florida. Walt Disney World was inviting the world media to Orlando to celebrate the sixtieth anniversary of Mickey Mouse and Mark knew who to call. He did, and we went! The March 20, 1989, edition of *Live at 5* was the first news programme in the world to originate live, and in its entirety, from Walt Disney World. It was quite an education for everyone involved, particularly Nancy Regan, who had yet to experience a "Celebrate the Maritimes" kind of remote broadcast. And getting there was part of the adventure.

Nancy and I flew to Boston with Paul Mennier, who was on his way to the Blue Jays' spring training camp in Dunedin, Florida. We ended up spending the evening of St. Patrick's Day in Boston, soaking up the Celtic celebrations in America's most Irish city. The next morning, we headed out to Orlando as first-class guests of Delta Airlines, arriving at the palatial Grand Floridian hotel in time to narrate two stories about Walt Disney World and its history, which Mark Campbell had shot and written, and was ready to produce. Richard Zurawski was already in Florida working with producer Jocelyn Corkum and cameraman Pat Kennedy on the pilot for a children's science series tentatively titled *WOW!* (World of Wonder). Later, as *Wonder Why?*, it was picked up and aired nationally on the CTV Network and around the world in syndication.

Dick Prat was there as executive producer of both projects (and it didn't rain). The day of our historic live remote broadcast was so hot and sunny our makeup melted on the way to the location, which was just opposite the Italian pavilion at Epcot Centre. That wasn't a problem though, since Disney generously furnished each of us with an astheticist, who expertly applied more types of makeup than I had ever seen, then dutifully mopped our lightly perspiring brows.

LIVE AT DISNEYWORLD! The ATV team at EPCOT in 1989. Left to right, Disney Canada's Carla Sagato, Producer Mark Campbell, Richard Zurawski, Steve Murphy, Disney's "Backdoor" Tony Howard, Nancy Regan, News Director Dick Prat, and Director Jocelyn Corkum.

The "crew" Disney supplied for our remote consisted of three cameramen, a floor director, a lighting technician, an audio operator, a couple of grips and gaffers (technicians), and a director. A lighting director rode in on a golf cart, and strode around our set with his light meter, pronouncing it in need of supplementary lighting: two fifty-thousand-watt giants. We were skeptical about the need to add "fill" to a brilliant Florida day, but when we saw the tapes later there was no doubt the extra lights really made the picture sparkle. Working with the Disney crew was an education in the big time way of doing things. We weren't allowed to so much as look at a piece of equipment, let alone touch it, and the way the whole thing was stage-managed was simply astonishing. Wranglers moved Mickey Mouse and the other Disney characters around with all of the precision and firm efficiency of secret service agents guarding the president of the United States. They even spoke into unseen microphones up their sleeves while monitoring radio transmissions on secret-agent-style ear pieces. The arrival of "The Mouse" at our location was co-ordinated to the second so that he wouldn't be seen in two places at once. (Our Disney escorts explained that since there was only one Mickey,

SEVERAL MEMBERS of the twenty-person Disney technical crew assigned to *Live at 5.*

JOCELYN CORKUM AND MARK CAMPBELL (right) directed and produced the first live news broadcast in the world to originate from Disneyworld.

NANCY GETS A BIRTHDAY SURPRISE from the "master of the house of mouse."

they didn't want children hearing that he had been seen at one end of the park while they had seen him at the other). In person, Mickey doesn't "speak," but he was nice enough to bring a cake for Nancy, who was celebrating her birthday.

The Florida show was Mark's first as a field producer, but he pulled it off with the skill of a seasoned veteran. After consulting with Dick, he wisely opted to put Jocelyn Corkum in the director's chair. The director furnished by Walt Disney World graciously stepped aside, recognizing that Jocelyn knew our format and he did not. She expertly called cameras in Orlando, while co-ordinating with the control room in Halifax. The hour went to air without a hitch—except when Walt Disney World's beautifully animated leader tape (the countdown from ten that precedes an item to be played back on the air) was accidentally aired as part of a story about the Magic Kingdom. Except with its lovely little musical soundtrack and shimmering images of Tinkerbell flitting over the fabled Cinderella's castle igniting multicoloured fireworks, it looked like it was supposed to be part of the story! Back at the station, no one even recognized the error and I suspect not many at-home viewers did either.

The Disney people were greatly impressed with our history-making show. When we all adjourned to a bar at the Polynesian resort, one of the Disney technicians quizzed us about job opportunities back at ATV. Nancy and I flew out to Boston that evening by way of wicked thunderstorms and a strange coincidence in Atlanta. Boarding our Delta jetliner at Hartsfield International Airport, I found a man already sitting in my seat. Anxious to prevent a scene, a flight attendant hustled down the narrow aisle and asked each of us to produce our boarding passes. To her surprise (and mine and his), we had both been assigned the same seat...because we both had the same name! People for several rows behind us and in front of us looked on in amused amazement after overhearing that there were two Steve Murphys assigned to the same seat. The passengers erupted in outright howls of laughter when it turned out the woman I was traveling with was named Nancy Regan (Regan sounded like Reagan to their southern ears). The next day, we returned to Halifax in a miserable March snowstorm without having to do much explaining to the customs officers at the airport; they knew where we had been.

It would be the fall before Mark Campbell had a chance to spread his wings again. However, three months later, Nancy and I were back in an amusement park: Upper Clements Park, in Clementsport, Nova Scotia, which was surrounded by controversy because of the amount of money John Buchanan's government had spent building it. We were there for the official opening day—June 23—to launch the third season of a considerably scaled back "Celebrate the Maritimes." The charter aircraft and motor home were gone, as were several of our technicians and one of our co-hosts, but the spirit was as strong as ever. Several of the shows from that third, abbreviated season rank among the best of the "Celebrate" series, most notably the unforgettable "Beach Boys on the Beach."

Mark Kliffer and Donald Tarlton knew each other as kids growing up in Montreal. By the mid-1970s, Mark was Mark Lee, programme director at CFBC Radio in Saint John, and Donald was Donald K. Donald, concert promoter extraordinaire. Mark was also doing some concert promoting as something of a Maritime point man for his childhood friend. Years earlier, as student council president, I had a number of business dealings with Mark, who leased the Saint John High School auditorium for concerts by artists like Valdy and Dan Hill, and hired "student police" to work security. By the late eighties Mark had moved into the big time with another Saint Johnner named Jack Livingstone in a business called Major Concerts International (MCI). It was Jack who called me in the spring of 1989 with word of what he confidently predicted would be the biggest show the Maritimes had ever seen. "Just imagine, Murph," he purred "the Beach Boys, on the Beach, at Parlee Beach."

It didn't take much imagining. I had seen the Beach Boys in concert in a jam-packed Halifax Metro Centre, where crazed fans of "the never ending summer" had spent two hours singing and dancing and spiking beach balls. Recreating that scene on the Maritimes' best and most popular beach seemed like simple

DIRECTOR JOCELYN CORKUM, Camerman Paul Creelman (left), and another member of the crew grapple with technical difficulties backstage at soggy Parlee Beach in 1989.

genius. Jack and Mark were hoping *Live at 5* would provide coverage of the announcement of the big event, and help promote ticket sales. In exchange, we were given virtually unlimited access to the concert venue on the weekend of the event. The promoters also promised to give us an exclusive interview with the Beach Boys. The concert was to be held on Canada Day, which in 1989 fell on a Sunday. Since there was no *Live at 5* that day, we decided to produce a "Celebrate the Maritimes" show on tape, and play it back the next day.

The Shediac area was warm and sunny and already jammed with vehicles and people when our caravan pulled in around noon on Saturday, the day before the concert. True to their word, Jack and Mark gave us the run of the place: backstage, all access passes for our staff, and great locations for our vehicles, satellite truck, and cameras. They also arranged for me to sit down with Beach Boys Mike Love, Al Jardine, and Bruce Johnston that evening at Hotel Beausejour in Moncton. It was an experience to meet and speak with these musical legends, particularly Love, who was one of the founders of the band. He had a certain celebrity smugness about him, undoubtedly the product of

"WELCOME TO PARTY BEACH!" Nancy Regan and Steve Murphy greet a crowd of sixty-eight thousand as they host *Live at 5* from Shediac, New Brunswick, in July 1989.

years in the spotlight on and off stage. It also seemed disappointingly obvious to me that for Love, performing had long since become just a job. That impression was borne out the next day during the concert, when more than one observer speculated that Love and the others were lip-syncing the words to at least some of their summer anthems, including their then monster-hit "Kokomo."

Mark Lee and Jack Livingstone chose to stage the "Beach Boys on the Beach" on the Canada Day weekend at least in part because it was the most reliable weekend of the summer, weatherwise. History suggested rain was highly unlikely. History was wrong. The day of the show, it poured for hours. It was a driving, heavy rain—the kind that soaks you to the soul, the kind that fell on the day John Hughes came home. Most of the almost seventy thousand fans didn't seem to mind. Some had come prepared with big umbrellas and raincoats; many others purchased green garbage bags from enterprising merchants who popped up at the site. Most simply decided to get good and wet.

It was a motley mob that greeted Nancy and me when we took the stage to kick off the show with the words "Welcome to Party

Drenched New Brunswick premier Frank McKenna is interviewed by Steve Murphy backstage at "Beach Boys on the Beach."

Singin' (and dancin') in the rain! Beach Boys founding member Mike Love asks Nancy to dance!

Beach"! We used that sequence to start the "Celebrate the Maritimes" show that aired the following night. The remainder of the programme was made up of segments we recorded during and mostly after the concert. We were allowed to air several excerpts from the concert itself, including one in which Nancy was waltzed around the stage by Mike Love to the strains of "Surfer Girl'! A drenched Frank McKenna appeared on the show, basking in the glow of all the great publicity New Brunswick was getting in the world media. The province had hired a helicopter and camera crew to shoot aerials of the huge crowd on the beach, and of course we were feeding news footage out to the Maritimes on ATV and across Canada on CTV.

The rain caused some technical difficulties and putting it all together later turned out to be a real problem too. I had come down with near pneumonia and wasn't able to work on the post-production—that task fell to Jocelyn and videotape editor Steve Rafuse, who started but couldn't finish the show that night, working as they were in the back of a badly lit and damp production truck. They were back at it early the following morning, but the editing was not finished in time for the tapes to be

Drier times. Nancy and Steve live on the waterfront in Yarmouth.

transported back to Halifax to be played back, as we had planned. Instead, with just over an hour to spare, we headed by car to CKCW-TV in Moncton, arriving just in time to load the tapes into a tape player and cue Halifax master control to take "the feed." We were back at Shediac in time to watch the final few minutes of the show on a black and white monitor, surrounded by a crew of tired technicians who by then were enjoying an ice cold beer on a sunny and balmy July afternoon. The great weather had arrived... one day late.

There were a several other memorable "Celebrate the Maritimes" shows that summer, including one in Greenfield, Queens County, Nova Scotia, where we covered pole climbing, axe throwing, and log rolling at the International Woodsmen's Competition. That, it turned out, was also the very last, regularly scheduled "Celebrate" show. There were other summer remotes, but none involved the large road shows of those first three seasons. It was a magical time that produced some entertaining, unscripted live television. Most people who worked on some or any of those programmes will now tell you that the shows themselves were something to celebrate!

Talking Politics

THE BEGINNING OF MY TENURE hosting *Live at 5* coincided roughly with major political changes in the province of New Brunswick. After seventeen years, and one too many scandals, Richard Hatfield's Conservatives were on their last legs. A young lawyer from Chatham named McKenna was deliberately keeping a low profile, waiting to present himself as Liberal premier-in-waiting when Hatfield called an election, which he finally did in the late summer of 1987.

From the outset, Frank McKenna knew he was going to win and win big. Opinion polls suggested the Conservatives were in deep trouble everywhere in the province, even in Hatfield's native Carleton County. McKenna's campaign strategy was simple and effective: present himself and the Liberal party as a modest, fresh, and credible alternative. The McKenna who appeared in a *Live at 5* interview days before the 1987 election was remarkably earnest and optimistic. He also exuded a sort of provincial patriotism that contrasted starkly with Hatfield's "just because I'm premier doesn't mean I want to live here" attitude. McKenna projected an obstinate determination to make New Brunswick a better place. The subtext brilliantly communicated throughout that campaign and in the early months of his first term was that New Brunswick had become "second rate" under Hatfield and that New Brunswickers were suffering from low esteem as a result.

McKenna was cast as the champion of the underdog province and the man who could voice its concerns. He didn't make many specific promises—he didn't have to. But one thing he did tell me he would do was press for unspecified changes in the Meech Lake Constitutional Accord, which Hatfield and all of the other premiers had signed earlier and promised to ratify by June of 1990. McKenna's intention to review the deal proved the beginning of the end of Meech Lake. New Brunswick later embraced most of the accord and encouraged holdouts, like Clyde Wells's Newfoundland, to do the same, but by then the damage was done. And as far as many in Quebec are concerned, McKenna was the first federalist to abandon Meech Lake. It is a reputation that haunts him to this day and could cost him a chance at the top job in Canadian politics.

The day after his election shut-out Frank McKenna made one other statement, one he quickly came to regret. During a *Live at 5* "two-way" (an interview in which the interviewee is in another place listening to questions in an earphone), the premier-designate said he thought ten years in office should be about long enough for any politician. For a man yet to take the oath of office, ten years must have seemed like an eternity. It probably seemed like a politically correct commitment, coming as it did on the heels of Hatfield's seventeen years, which almost everyone agreed was too long. But what McKenna did that day was start a clock that his opponents and reporters like me kept an eye on. By 1992, it was generally accepted that McKenna was halfway through his self-imposed term. In the fall of 1996, I requested and was granted a wide-ranging sit-down interview with McKenna to mark the beginning of his tenth year—implicitly, the beginning of the end. During the interview McKenna conceded that he regretted making the ten year comment, which by then was commonly understood to have been a promise, although at no time in my memory did Frank McKenna ever say

FRANK
McKENNA at
ATV's twenty-
fifth anniversary
celebration in
Moncton (1997).
He resigned as
premier a few
weeks later.

he would stay no longer than ten years. He might have opted to make the case that since no official promise had ever been made, he could stick around as premier as long as he wanted. He chose instead to do the wise and honourable thing: he resigned in October 1997 after exactly ten years in office. If anything, McKenna left before his time, adding further lustre to his already well-polished image as a new breed of politician. This "just plain Frank" image was already being cultivated in early 1988, when Dick Prat and I flew to Fredericton for a meeting with the rookie premier. He impressed and surprised us, showing up by himself (the masterful Maurice Robichaud had yet to join the premier's staff as communications director), on a Saturday afternoon with the keys to the front door of the Centennial Building. He led us to his office, where he listened to several programme proposals. After quizzing us about each of them, he decisively rejected the one that would have cost him money, and accepted the two that required only his time.

One of the programmes he agreed to be part of was a unique "Letters to the Premier" column to be aired on *Live at 5*. The idea was simple. Since the people of New Brunswick had not elected any opposition politicians to hold McKenna's Liberals accountable, we would allow the people to have a question period with their new premier on television. We received dozens of letters, covering issues ranging from healthcare to bilingualism, and Premier McKenna sat before a live camera one evening answering several of them. Although he answered "Letters to the Premier" questions only once, Frank McKenna remained remarkably accessible for his entire tenure as premier.

Seven years as host of *Live at 5* provided me the rare opportunity to meet and speak with virtually every other major political leader, provincial and federal, of the time, including the man who was prime minister for most of it. Brian Mulroney was extremely gracious, disarmingly so. He always had a kind word, prompted no doubt by one of his multitude of handlers. His voice was so deep and round that you could almost feel him speaking. He was quick to use humour or a chuckle to diffuse something he did not wish to discuss (personal matters, corruption, and his own increasing unpopularity), which came off looking somewhat devious on television. I am convinced it contributed to the intense personal dislike that many Canadians developed for the man. Mulroney was the perfect gentleman before and after, if not always during an interview. He did not hesitate to strike back when he disapproved of a question. On two occasions, exchanges that began with a smiling Mulroney chatting with me as "Steve" ended with a stern Mulroney addressing me as "Mr. Murphy." All was forgiven when the lights were turned off, and on both occasions, the prime minister sent me photographs of our interview, the second set inscribed with a kind message. Brian Mulroney may have been a crafty political operator (he did, after all, cut his teeth at St. Francis Xavier and grew up in the backrooms), but I suspect he was sincere in his belief that what he did was best for Canada.

John Turner became prime minister of Canada after waiting in the wings for a decade for Pierre Elliott Trudeau to take his final curtain call. During that time, Turner was mythologized by the media and romanticized by members of the Liberal Party, who didn't seem to realize that all that time off stage might make

BRIAN
MULRONEY meets
Nancy Regan
just before a *Live
at 5* interview,
October 14,
1988.

a fellow forget his lines. The John Turner who returned to the national spotlight in 1984 couldn't possibly live up to his advance billing. Not having played the part of a public figure since the mid-seventies, he was rusty and it showed. The media, which had earlier portrayed Turner as the blue-eyed saviour of the Liberal party, quickly seized on his obvious discomfort and began raising questions about whether he was the same charismatic young man people remembered. At no time was it more obvious that he wasn't the same man than when he patted Liberal Party president Iona Campagnola on the "behind" during a campaign stop. What might have passed for jocularity in the seventies was quickly condemned as blatant chauvinism in the more politically-correct eighties. His fashion sense was also seriously out of date. Turner campaigned in three-button blazers that in 1984 looked ten years behind the times.

The John Turner I encountered in the VIP lounge at Halifax International Airport in the fall of 1986 was smiling and good-natured; he shook my hand and offered me a beer. He seemed to have overcome the humiliation of the 1984 general election, which he lost, and was already looking forward to having

another crack at Brian Mulroney. John Turner struck me that day
as a man who no longer felt he had to live up to his own pre-
1984 press clippings. It was the confident and passionate Turner
whose greatest hour would come during the celebrated 1988
leader's debate on the issue of free trade. He lost the ensuing
election but won the respect and the votes of millions of
Canadians, particularly Atlantic Canadians. The Liberals made
a strong showing in all four eastern provinces.

My October 27, 1988, interview with Turner engendered
more hostile reaction than anything else I have ever done on television. We received hundreds of phone calls and dozens of letters, most laced with vitriol of the sort I had never experienced.
The interview was decidedly tough, perhaps too tough. It began
with questions about the sudden resignation of a Toronto Liberal
candidate who was suffering from a serious medical problem.
The persistence of my questioning clearly offended many viewers, as did subsequent queries about Jean Chretien, who had lost
the leadership to Turner and was widely seen as not doing much
to support him during the campaign. Senator Al Graham, the
wily Cape Bretoner traveling with Turner, was among the furi-
ous. He accused me of asking dirty questions in what looked to
him like a setup. In hindsight, I realize the criticisms were a
forerunner: Maritimers had already decided to support John
Turner. On election day, while Mulroney won the country,
Turner won the region.

A few years later, Jean Chretien won every seat in Atlantic
Canada with the exception of Saint John, where not even Brian
Mulroney's unpopularity or Kim Campbell's botched campaign
could dissuade people from voting for Elsie Wayne. So confident were the Liberals of their electoral success in the Maritimes
that ATV News was not able to get an interview with Jean
Chretien during the 1993 election campaign.

History was set to repeat itself in the 1997 campaign, until
the Grits, seeing their Maritime fortress beginning to crumble,
decided to grant Paul Mennier an eleventh-hour conversation
via satellite. It didn't make much difference. The Liberals were
wiped out in Nova Scotia, suffering losses to the NDP and the

FREQUENT
VISITOR JOE
CLARK chats with
Bruce Graham
on the way into a
mid-eighties *Live
at 5* interview.

…and with Paul
Mennier a
decade later.

PCs. A handful of New Brunswick Liberals were also defeated. Since then, I have had two extensive interviews with Jean Chrétien. Those who underestimate him do so at their own peril. The Prime Minister has supreme confidence in his political instincts, which have so far proven almost infallible. His handling of the 1996 Quebec Referendum was an obvious and disturbing exception. Frank McKenna once told me that Jean Chrétien has a sort of political antenna that helps him quickly size up almost every situation. Whatever his secret weapon, Jean Chrétien has enjoyed greater electoral success than any prime minister since Mackenzie King.

John Buchanan has his share of critics these days. The long-serving, free-spending former PC premier of Nova Scotia is often blamed for the serious financial problems from which the province has yet to recover. One seldom hears the governing PCs of today even mention his name, although he led the party for almost twenty years, winning four consecutive majority governments—a feat that, to my knowledge, can be claimed by no other living Canadian politician.

Buchanan was dismissed by his opponents as a lightweight when he first ran for premier as "Honest John" in the 1974 election that returned Gerry Regan for a second term. And in 1978, staunch and over-confident Liberals believed Buchanan would be relegated to the margins of history after losing to Regan a second time. But he didn't lose, mostly because he didn't rest after his first defeat. The Spryfield populist spent virtually every night and weekend between the 1974 and 1978 elections shaking hands, slapping backs, and kissing babies at church socials, community picnics, fairs, exhibitions, and parades all across Nova Scotia. So when voters angry with Regan's Liberals over skyrocketing power prices began looking around at the alternatives, they looked to "Honest John." A surprising number had met Buchanan and liked him. They were also willing to vote for him, and they did—over and over again.

And that is the essential truth about John M. Buchanan: he is a very likeable man, a charmer. His policies were somehow never as important to the voters as his personality. Some would argue that his policies were never really seriously scrutinized by many in the electorate, that he ran his election campaigns like popularity contests. That certainly was the case in his own riding of Halifax Atlantic, which included Lieblin Park, the neighbourhood where John and Mavis Buchanan still live. There, it was no secret that the former premier (and now senator) puts more stock in what he hears from the people he meets at the corner store than in what he reads in the papers. John Buchanan's sense of what is important to the public has always come from the public. And that is why he was such a good guest on my 1980's CJCH radio phone-in show. He was one of the first, if not the first, Canadian premier to regularly subject himself to the phone-in format. When I inherited *Hotline* from Dave Wright in 1981, it was already well established that the premier would appear at least twice a year. All it usually took to arrange the fall and spring visits was a quick call to the affable John O'Brien, the former *Chronicle-Herald* and CBC journalist who became the premier's long-serving press secretary. O'Brien later returned to journalism as news director at MITV and is now the communications director for the Halifax Regional Municipality.

On the day of the agreed-to appearance, John would arrive around 8:45 A.M. and spend the next fifteen minutes pacing the narrow hallway in the old CJCH Radio building, waiting for "The Boss" to arrive, which he always did with just seconds to spare. Then, the premier of Nova Scotia would sit on the other side of the microphone, willing to answer virtually anything he was asked. I usually started with a few questions about the issue of the day: the offshore, the deficit, the mandatory seat belt law. Then I would throw open the phone lines. There were always scores of calls, some from disgruntled voters and obvious political partisans looking to score points. But most of the people who called John Buchanan on the air were looking for help cutting through the red tape of government. They asked him to review their unsuccessful pleas to the transportation department for pavement on their dirt road, a sidewalk, or a gutter. They lobbied him to intervene with the then provincially owned electrical utility for a new power pole. Buchanan always listened intently and usually sympathetically, asking a few questions and then instructing O'Brien, who was on the other side of the glass in the control room, to get the caller's number for later follow-up. I frequently appealed to callers and listeners, asking them to call me if the premier didn't get back to them. Several did call me later to say that Buchanan had solved their problem or had at least tried to. I never once heard back from someone who had not had his or her call returned. On the air, the premier was seldom berated for his position on any issue, and always remained the picture of calm when he was.

John Buchanan also has a tremendous sense of humour, which was a lucky thing for Bruce Graham and me after an unfortunate and celebrated "blooper" during ATV's 1984 Nova Scotia election coverage. Our live coverage of the returns included a live camera inside the Buchanans's Spryfield home. The idea was that we could watch the premier and his family as they watched the results pour in, and speak to Buchanan as soon as the outcome was clear. When our decision desk, led by unflappable assignment editor and political sage John Soosaar, declared the Buchanan Tories headed for a third consecutive majority government, we anxiously called for our live shot. But when we spun around in our chairs to watch the premier's reaction, what we saw on the large television screen between us instead was a large squealing pig.

"That is obviously not Premier John Buchanan," Bruce Graham deadpanned after a moment of stunned silence. Reporter Rick Grant, who was stationed outside the premier's home, says he could clearly hear John Buchanan's howls of laughter.

Technical difficulties don't always produce such a light-hearted response from those on the receiving end. The late Joe Ghiz grew so frustrated during a *Live at 5* appearance in the late eighties that he actually stood up to leave during a live interview. The former premier was sitting in front of reporter Dan Viau's camera in our tiny Charlottetown newsroom, hearing my questions through a supposedly invisible earphone—the sort once used to listen to transistor radios. A couple of minutes into our conversation, the premier, who had been fidgeting with the earpiece, finally erupted in exasperation, saying that he simply couldn't "stand this thing anymore." From off-camera, Dan Viau quietly reminded him that we were on the air live, and the premier somehow managed to continue.

I was most impressed with a young man who appeared on *Live at 5* while serving in Brian Mulroney's cabinet as Minister of Youth. He was, in fact, at that time the youngest federal cabinet minister in history. Jean Charest was quick on his feet in both official languages, which he spoke beautifully and with an ease reminiscent of Pierre Trudeau. Now leader of the Quebec Liberal Party, Charest lost the leadership of his Progressive Conservative Party to Kim Campbell in 1993, only to be drafted into the job after the Tory monolith was reduced to two just seats in the 1993 election. Jean Charest sat in one of those seats; Elsie Wayne was in the other.

Elsie just might be the best grassroots politician I have ever encountered. Her political career was getting started right around the time I was cutting my teeth in the news business. As a young radio reporter, I interviewed Elsie Wayne often in her capacity as the plain-speaking chair of the "Glen Falls Flood Committee." She and her group were fighting for and eventually got a solution to the persistent problem of flooding in their low-lying East Saint John neighbourhood. By the time the 1977 municipal election rolled around, Elsie was a household name around Saint John. She had no trouble winning a seat on Common Council, where she quickly developed a reputation for outspoken honesty and tenacity that eventually led to her becoming a candidate for the mayoralty in 1983. She ran against incumbent Bob Lockhart (who gave me my first job in radio), who had won the job in 1980 on a promise to build a civic centre, a promise he had not been able to keep (Harbour Station came much later).

Lockhart was trying to become the first mayor in Saint John's two-hundred-year history to be elected to consecutive terms, something he had tried unsuccessfully a decade earlier, after his first term as mayor. His luck was no better in 1983. It was Elsie Wayne who would later break the consecutive-term hex, winning not two or three but four consecutive mandates from the people of her "Greatest Little City in the East." By 1993, the popular mayor must have seemed a dream candidate for the federal Conservatives, who were looking for new faces, particularly female faces, to help reshape the party's image (and help people forget about Mulroney, the GST, and free trade). On Election Day, Elsie delivered, although she and Charest were the only two Tories who did.

I had covered Elsie Wayne for several years before realizing she was Richard "Buzzy" Wayne's wife. As a child, "Buzzy" was an important figure in my mind: he was the man who fixed the TV! That my parents knew "Buzzy" well and Elsie somewhat did not really become clear to me until June 1988 as several of us walked down Prince William Street in Saint John, following my address to the Saint John High graduation class. I had been invited to speak on the tenth anniversary of my own graduation, and the mayor was a platform guest. She responded loudly and good-naturedly to some of my comments. Thereafter, the family connection established, Elsie Wayne became something of a *Live at 5* booster, not to mention a remarkably engaging occasional guest. Elsie interviews were always energetic and a source of great amusement for my colleagues—not so much because Elsie's answers were funny but because she almost always called me "Stephen." I began my radio career as Stephen Murphy, which is after all the name that's on my birth certificate and the name by which I was known through school. It was CFBC news director Daryl Good (known during his radio years in Saint John as Robert Phillips), who suggested that I go by "Steve." The name stuck professionally; about the only people who call me Stephen are relatives, close friends, and Elsie. I mentioned this to her about ten years ago, good-naturedly and only half seriously, but she got the message and hasn't called me Stephen since. Now, I'm Stevie!

When it comes to talking politics, nobody does it better than Mike Duffy. The affable Prince Edward Islander has covered Parliament Hill for thirty years while keeping a finger on the

FLOOR DIRECTOR
MIKE TRENCHARD
adjusts a battery
pack during a
live interview
with then-mayor
Elsie Wayne in
Saint John,
August 1987.

political pulse here in the Maritimes. He does it by staying in touch with a list of contacts longer than his cell phone bill. For years, Mike was a CBC star, first on radio, then on television. When Mike decided to leave the CBC in 1988 for his own hour-long weekly current affairs programme, he was without question one of the corporation's most popular personalities.

Sunday Edition was produced at Ottawa CTV affiliate CJOH. ATV was one of a number of local stations that agreed to participate with CJOH-owner Baton Broadcasting in the production of the programme. That meant Mike Duffy was, at least nominally, an ATV personality. Almost immediately, he began appearing on *Live at 5's* regular Friday political segment. Dave Wright had started the "Ottawa Report" years earlier, chatting each week with ATV Ottawa bureau chief Ken Lawrence. Dave knew that hardcore politics didn't always make for good television, so the Friday segment was always heavy on insider information, and informal in its presentation. The feature and the approach continued when I moved to *Live at 5*. A short time later Ken Lawrence left journalism to work for the PC government of the day. He was replaced by Ken MacDonald in a segment from and about "inside Ottawa." Ken, who had worked at Halifax radio station CHNS in the 1970s, knew the Maritimes well, and usually enriched his weekly segments with local references. Even as vice-president of national news for Global Television, Ken still marvels at just how well recognized he was in the Maritimes as a political commentator on ATV.

The addition of Mike Duffy to an already-successful segment made it even more popular. "Duff's" knowledge of politics and the region is unequaled. He has been a frequent participant in ATV election coverage over the years, and was kind enough to include me as an occasional participant on his wildly popular political panel on *Sunday Edition*. We continued working together on *Live at 5's* Friday segment even after Dave Wright retired and I moved to the anchor desk. These days, Mike is a mainstay on CTV's *Newsnet*. Our Friday feature, now dubbed "Mike Duffy on Parliament Hill," moved to *The ATV Evening News* in the spring of 2000, when the programme expanded to its current one-hour format. Well-informed, well respected, and well loved, Mike Duffy is one of a kind.

Star Struck

LIVE AT 5'S INSATIABLE APPETITE for entertainment stories has led to dozens of interviews with some of the biggest names in show business. Many have been conducted at posh hotels in Los Angeles and New York on junkets bankrolled by movie companies. These "interview factories" and the people who take part in them are often criticized—unjustly in my estimation. While it is true the movie studios hope to influence positive reviews for their films, I can honestly say I was never once told what to say or chastised for what I chose to say about a film or a star. Nor did a movie ever buy its way onto *Live at 5*. In the early days, we ran items about the big shows and the big stars from ABC, CBS, or another of the entertainment "feeds" we subscribed to. Given the choice, we have always felt it is better to have ATV personalities ask the questions and decide which answers to use. A practice that began with Nancy Regan and me has continued with entertainment reporters Joanne Nugent, Todd Battis, and MairiAnna Bachynsky.

Many of the superstars I met and interviewed during these junkets seemed bored with and in some cases hostile toward the whole process. No wonder—they were expected to sit in a hotel and pleasantly answer the same, often silly questions over and over again from a steady stream of inquisitors whose hometowns included such places as Cheyenne, Wyoming, and Halifax, Nova Scotia!

Over the years, I was privileged to sit down face-to-face with a number of big stars, among them Oscar-winner Anjelica Houston and the late Raul Julia (on a junket for their funny and clever *Addams Family*), and the intelligent and alluring Annette Bening and Harrison Ford in a so-so movie called *Regarding Henry*. Both Bening and Ford were gracious and friendly, prompting my early impression that the biggest stars are often the nicest and least affected by their considerable fame. Sally Field confirmed the theory—I really liked her. Several actors I interviewed as supporting players are now getting top billing: the talented Willem Dafoe starred in a terrible Vietnam picture called *Flight of the Intruder;* an ingenue named Elizabeth Shue went on to win hearts and critical reviews in *Leaving Las Vegas*; and a noticeably troubled and distracted Robert Downey Junior was about to be nominated for an academy award for his brilliant performance as Charles Chaplin.

Nancy Regan has turned in a number of unforgettable interviews with stars over the years. One of her earliest was nothing short of a Hollywood coup. As the newly-minted co-host of *Live at 5*, Nancy managed to land the only major television interview with Kirk Douglas while he was shooting a made-for-TV film (*The Secret*) on the south shore of Nova Scotia. Getting onto the set took determination and patience and when the venerable actor finally appeared for the promised interview, he didn't have much to say…but he said it only to Nancy Regan on *Live at 5*. Persistence also helped Nancy land an exclusive interview with Donald Sutherland. The Saint-John-born, Bridgewater-raised actor was back in Nova Scotia in the early nineties shooting a film, but was "definitely not granting any interviews," and certainly not any local interviews. Not willing to accept no for an answer, Nancy and a camera crew headed to the film's shooting location. Once there, a security guard assured them that yes, Mr. Sutherland was there, and no, he wasn't giving any interviews.

NANCY REGAN
WITH PAUL
"CROCODILE
DUNDEE" HOGAN
during a junket
in Los Angeles.

Nancy prevailed on the guard, a *Live at 5* viewer, to pass on her business card, which contained a quickly scrawled personal note on the back. The guard returned a few minutes later, dumbfounded, with word that Mr. Sutherland would agree to an interview after all. It seems years earlier Donald Sutherland had shadowed a sports reporter by the name of Gerry "Gabby" Regan, who had given the youngster a chance to take the microphone. Many years later, the superstar Sutherland returned the favour.

Occasionally, a big star joins us for an interview "in the flesh." Such encounters usually make for pretty good television and are sometimes also personally gratifying. I got to meet one of my favourite actors in a one-on-one interview on *Live at 5*. Ed Asner starred in what I still consider two of the best television series of all time—*The Mary Tyler Moore Show*, the brilliant seventies comedy series in which Asner played irascible news producer Lou Grant, and *Lou Grant*, the subsequent dramatic series that saw a more serious Grant running the city room of the fictional Los Angeles Tribune newspaper. I had seen virtually every episode of both programmes and was a big Asner

NANCY WITH
GARTH BROOKS
after an Eastern
Canada exclusive
interview in
Montreal, 1995.

fan, so when it was announced that he was to appear at Dalhousie
University in support of one of his left-wing causes, we booked
him for an interview. When it was over, on a whim, I invited
him to a late dinner with my then wife and friends Gordon
Proudfoot and Madine van der Plaat. To my surprise and our
great pleasure, he accepted and that evening Stephen Risley and
his staff at Ryan Duffy's served up a sumptuous meal of mostly steak and lobster to the star and the star struck. Edward Asner
proved an engaging and modest man who generously shared
stories about his career and his causes, including an amusing
anecdote about Mary Tyler Moore's shriek of glee when she and
her producer/husband Grant Tinker auditioned Asner for the
role of Lou Grant.

Vanna White turned more than a few heads when she joined us
for a *Live at 5* interview. *The Wheel of Fortune* letter-turner was
brought to the Maritimes in the early nineties by the Atlantic
Lottery Corporation to host a big money giveaway being produced
in the studio next to the newsroom. Almost everyone recognized
her famous face instantly but many who met her seemed surprised
when she spoke: she was smart, articulate, and charming.

THE LATE "OUTLAW" Waylon Jennings on the set with Nancy and the children of ATV employees, listening to songs from his children's album.

Of all of the celebrity interviews I have ever conducted, one with Oprah Winfrey prompted the greatest response from the general public. Her highly successful and groundbreaking talk show originally aired in Atlantic Canada on ATV's sister station ASN, at 5:00 P.M. Nancy and I quickly recognized *The Oprah Winfrey Show* as the most strenuous competition *Live at 5* had ever faced, and began quietly lobbying Dick Prat and Joe Irvine to move the show, preferably to ATV. Our furtive pleas went largely unheeded even when the four o'clock timeslot opened up after MITV snatched the powerhouse daytime drama *General Hospital* away from CTV. *Santa Barbara*, the soap that replaced *General Hospital,* was not a ratings winner, despite intense promotion on ATV and NBC, the originating US network. Faced with an under performer as *Live at 5's* lead-in show, and worried about the impact that might have on the newscast and subsequently in prime time, Dick and Joe decided to move *The Oprah Winfrey Show*.

Part of the strategy to promote the change called for having Oprah appear on *Live at 5*. Her producers were more than willing to have Nancy or me travel to Chicago to sit down with the reigning queen of daytime, but that's not what we had in mind. ATV promotions director Anne Marie Varner instead requested a live, half-hour interview via satellite from the HARPO studios in Chicago. It was a bold demand to make, so we were pleasantly surprised when word blew in from the windy city that Oprah had agreed to our request. One of the reasons she agreed, it later turned out, was that Varner, who really knew how to pitch an idea, had sent Oprah's producers a copy of a *TV Guide* cover story that had proclaimed *Live at 5* Canada's most popular newscast. The claim was not inaccurate. In terms of ratings points (the measure of the percentage of a total population group watching a given programme), we were number one. Oprah Winfrey was and is a gifted television executive who certainly understands what ratings mean.

"You guys are smokin," she enthused minutes into our live interview, even if she wasn't quite sure exactly where we were. During the first commercial break she quizzed me about the geographic location of the Maritimes, and seemed somewhat surprised that there even was a place "east of Maine." For days afterward I was interrogated by dozens of people about "meeting Oprah." "What's she really like?" they wondered. My answer then, and now, is that she seems like a very nice and smart person, but of course while I did speak with the woman, I have only ever seen her on television. Nancy Regan, who later jetted to Chicago for a backstage look at the making of *The Oprah Winfrey Show* and an interview with Oprah, was most impressed with the woman, her production staff, and facilities.

Same with Howie Mandel: he's got to be the funniest man I've never met! The frantic funnyman was launching an Atlantic Canadian tour in St. John's, where ASN maintained a modest news bureau. Promoter Jack Livingstone offered me a chance to speak with Howie on the eve of his arrival in the Maritimes. The first few minutes of the "two-way" interview were pretty standard, but then Howie started playing with the "props" he was finding on and in reporter Allan Rowe's desk, including a roll of toilet tissue, which the comic quickly twisted around his head. He then announced that the "hundredth caller would be

WHEEL OF FORTUNE'S Vanna White with Steve Murphy.

chauffeured to his [Halifax] concert at station expense," and so on. His patter was so lightning-fast and hilarious, I was unable to get a word in—which was okay because I was laughing so hard I could hardly speak anyway.

The situation comedy *Full House* was a fixture on the ATV programme schedule for more than a decade. For several years, it aired six times a week: once in prime time and once each evening immediately following *The ATV Evening News*. For reasons the critics could never comprehend, it was a huge hit with families and particularly young children. The show made stars out of almost all of its cast members, but particularly Bob Saget (who went on to host *America's Funniest Home Videos*), the Olsen twins, and a young woman named Candace Cameron, who appeared on *Live at 5* for an interview with Paul and Nancy in the mid-nineties. No one really appreciated just how big a star she had become until the next day, when Dartmouth's Mic Mac Mall was mobbed by thousands of young fans anxious to catch a glimpse of the starlet during a public appearance.

ATV has always been in the forefront of promoting major entertainment events, and was the premiere sponsor when Bill

NANCY AND PAUL
with *Full House*
star Candace
Cameron.
Thousands of
fans later made
for a "full house"
at Dartmouth's
Mic Mac Mall.

Cosby played the Halifax Metro Centre in 1989. It was a natural fit. *The Cosby Show* was continuing its long run as television's number one programme, and was turning in fantastic ratings for ATV airing weeknights as well. So it was decided that Nancy and I should introduce the headliner. We arrived at the Metro Centre about an hour before show time for a backstage meeting with Cosby. He was positively charming, soft-spoken with the unmistakable aura of superstardom, without any of the pretense. His only advice for us novices was that we not try to be funny. Nancy and I got a warm response and a few chuckles from the capacity crowd but Bill Cosby brought the house down. And he didn't even have to try!

Back in the days when television was black and white and very local, a weekly show called *Hi Society* was a showcase for talented singers and vocal groups. My father, who is gifted with near-perfect pitch and is an excellent judge of musical talent, watched it regularly and would occasionally comment when someone really caught his fancy. That's how I first heard the name Anne Murray. She appeared on the show with a group from UNB and Dad confidently predicted big things for her.

"DON'T TRY TO BE FUNNY," advised Bill Cosby before Nancy and Steve introduced him to a sold-out Halifax Metro Centre in 1989.

Like most Maritimers, my family followed Anne's progress first on *Sing Along Jubilee* (the first must-see TV show in this part of the world), then as a recording artist. I have therefore been an Anne fan most of my life. So, when ATV announced it was sponsoring her 1990 homecoming concert at the Halifax Metro Centre, I proposed putting together a half-hour interview special with the Springhill songstress. The station loved the idea, and so did Leonard Rambeau, Anne's long-time manager and confidant.

I had never met Leonard but I knew all about him from his proud aunt, Georgina Briand. Not only did George and her husband Mike live down the street from my parents in Saint John, their niece Maddy Williams is one of my mother's best friends. As a child of ten or eleven years of age, I was impressed but perplexed when Georgina got a Christmas card from Anne Murray. "Snowbird" had just become the biggest selling Canadian single of all time, and was also burning up the charts in the United States, a major accomplishment in the days before Canadian content regulations for radio. Georgina had explained that her nephew, Leonard, was Anne's manager and that he had been responsible for the card. Over the years, I heard many other Anne and Leonard stories from Georgina, so by the time I placed a call to him to pitch my interview idea, I felt I knew who I was dealing with. And apparently, so did Leonard; he gave the proposal swift and favourable consideration. It was agreed that I would fly to Toronto and interview Anne at CITY-TV, which like ATV was owned by CHUM Limited. CITY agreed to provide a studio location and two cameramen for the shoot. Our news publicist, Paul Bowen, just happened to be home in Toronto on vacation, and was tapped to serve as field producer. During our conversation, Anne generously and humourously referred to Leonard as "my brain." It wasn't much of an exaggeration. Leonard managed Anne's life and career from her early days as a barefoot folksinger playing university cafés all the way to the glittering showrooms of the Las Vegas strip, with command performances for presidents and princes and a wall-full of gold records in between. He knew Anne inside out, and was very proud of her too. Chatting in the green room at CITY before our interview, he proposed that Anne Murray's was one of only two truly unique female voices in the world—Barbra Streisand's being the other.

Most amazing about the relationship between the two Nova Scotians—Leonard was from Smelt Brook, Cape Breton, and didn't mind telling you so—was that the only "contract" between them was one that had been hastily scribbled on the back of an envelope in the late sixties. It became the foundation for a management and entertainment corporation they later founded with Anne's husband, Bill Langstroth, a talented entertainer and producer in his own right.

Leonard stood quietly off camera as Anne and I chatted about her long and successful career. She reflected on her hits, the biggest of which was "You Needed Me" (not "Snowbird" as many of us assume). She also spoke about a song she wished she had recorded, "Somebody's Knockin," a 1981 country crossover monster-hit for Terry Gibbs.

She reminisced about her childhood in Springhill, swimming in Northumberland Strait ("we were never dumb enough to

ANNE MURRAY quizzes her long-time friend and manager, the late Leonard Rambeau (off camera), during an interview with Steve shot at Toronto's CITY-TV.

swim in the Bay of Fundy..."), and her early days as a performer, including an appearance in the late sixties on *Hi Society*. When asked about aspiring singers whose work she admired, she spoke with earnest enthusiasm about a young Quebec chanteuse named Celine Dion, for whom she predicted very big things. Back on the home front, she spoke with great pride about the Anne Murray Centre, which had opened a couple of years earlier. (ATV carried the opening ceremony live.)

"It's not a museum," she insisted. "Although my friends call me 'the museum piece'," she quipped. Later, I drove to Springhill with cameraman Paul Creelman to tape segments for the half-hour special with Anne. The show was well received, even by the star's charming mother, who stopped me at Anne's Halifax concert to say: "Thank you for such a nice interview with my daughter." That meant a lot to me.

The success of "A Conversation with Anne," as the programme was called, led to a similar show with Rita MacNeil, also aired as a prelude to an ATV-sponsored Maritime tour. The day Rita and I sat down for a chat at the Halifax Sheraton Hotel was the same day the singer confirmed she was ending her long-

ATV's JONATHAN KAY AND RON
SHAW reporting live from the opening
of the Anne Murray Centre in
Springhill, Nova Scotia, July 28,
1989.

SPRINGHILL VIA SATELLITE! July 1989.

standing relationship with manager Brookes Diamond. There
were already well-founded rumours suggesting Rita was about
to sign with Leonard Rambeau and Balmur, which she did a
short while later. In the meantime, Nancy Regan and I travelled
from city to city, introducing Rita to appreciative audiences in
sold-out hockey rinks all around the Maritimes.

Rita MacNeil really is one of the nicest people I have ever
met. Her speaking voice is as soft as her singing voice is powerful! A shy woman, she admits freely that she has to muster up
the courage to walk onto a stage. But once she's there, she
delights her listeners with a sincere and sensitive interpretation
of her songs, many of which are written in her mind before
being put to paper and eventually recorded. At the end of this
particular concert tour, Rita called Nancy and me backstage and
presented us with a small gift and a personal note, both of which
I still have. It is this sort of kindness and generosity of spirit
that many of Rita's fans recognize—perhaps subconsciously—
in her music. It is precisely because she really is the kind-heart-
ed soul she seems to be that so many of her fans were outraged
when some in the national media made insensitive inquiries

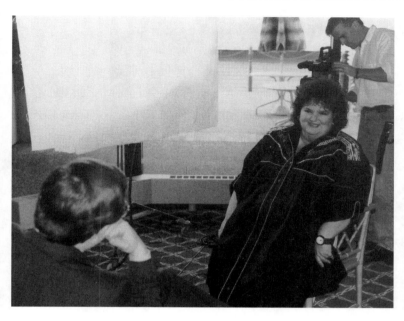

A CONVERSATION WITH RITA. Cameraman Carl Pomeroy shoots Steve as he chats with Rita MacNeil in the lobby of the Halifax Sheraton Hotel.

about her weight. And there were howls of protest from Rita MacNeil fans across the country when the CBC cancelled her 1990s variety show.

Nowhere are people more proud of Rita than in Big Pond, Cape Breton, a tiny hamlet on the shores of the Bras D'Or. Besides being Rita's hometown and the location of her now famous tea-room, Big Pond is also home to a summer music festival that draws thousands of people from near and far. Rita hadn't appeared at the festival for several seasons when she agreed to appear as a headliner in the summer of 1992. That sounded like a good reason to take *Live at 5* on the road again, so we did, originating the sixty minutes via satellite from a farmer's field. The festival organizers kindly allowed us to use their stage and public address system to involve the hundreds of fans who were camped out for the "concert under the stars." The centrepiece of our show was an interview, arranged by Leonard Rambeau, with the hometown star. I only saw Leonard once more after that sunny summer day in Cape Breton. Jocelyn and I were returning from the Bahamas, waiting out a storm at Toronto's Pearson Airport, when I spied Len waiting to board a

STEVE AND
NANCY welcome
the *Live at 5*
audience to The
Big Pond
Summer
Festival, 1992.

flight. We spoke briefly and later he sent me a copy of Anne Murray's *Croonin'*, a wonderful collection of the songs Anne grew up listening to. It was a very thoughtful gesture from a man who had so much on his mind: Len had been diagnosed with cancer and passed away several months later, many years too early.

The Saturday morning after Rita MacNeil's Big Pond home-coming concert, producer Ian Morrison and I headed back to Halifax by car. We left Sydney in plenty of time to rendezvous with ASN anchor Ron Kronstein in Plymouth, Nova Scotia, where we had a delivery to make and some people to thank.

Days of Hope & Despair

PLYMOUTH IS A PRETTY AND UNASSUMING LITTLE PLACE in Nova Scotia's Pictou County, fated to be forever remembered for one terrible event. The Westray mine was well known—some would say infamous—even before it exploded. There hadn't been a large-scale commercial coal mine in Pictou County since 1974, when the Drummond Mine closed, bringing to an end almost 170 years of mining. Westray was developed by politicians in a hurry to create jobs in an area of persistent and high unemployment. At the highest echelons of power, these politicians had a personal interest in Pictou County. Consider the facts: the prime minister of the day, Martin Brian Mulroney, was first elected to Parliament as MP for Central Nova, which included Pictou County. Elmer Mackay, who resigned his seat in 1983 so Mulroney could run in the resulting by-election, had been rewarded with a senior role in the Mulroney cabinet. Pictou County MLA Donald Cameron was Industry Minister in John Buchanan's Nova Scotia PC government, and became premier himself when Buchanan was appointed to the Senate. It is reasonable to believe that all of these men wanted to do what they could for the voters of Pictou County. As important as the jobs were, from the outset there were safety concerns among local experts who believed Westray's coal was simply too gassy or potentially explosive, and therefore too dangerous, to mine. Over the years, many men had been killed and injured working the world's largest coal seam, the Foord. Sadly, those concerns proved well founded.

At 5:18 on the morning of May 9, 1992, just a few days after Westray mine owners Curragh Resources received an international award for safety, and just eight months into its operation, the mine exploded. A spark of uncertain origin ignited methane gas that bathed the mine shafts, producing a powerful blast fueled by mounds of coal dust. It is likely that at least some of the few who heard the explosion or felt the resulting tremor immediately feared the worst; they may have intuitively known that lives had been lost. But what followed in the hours immediately after the explosion was a rescue mission, born of the belief, or perhaps just the need to believe, that some or maybe even all of the twenty-six men on shift had survived. That is the story that was already beginning to take shape when ATV's Dan MacIntosh arrived at the mine site about forty-five minutes after the explosion. Instantly recognizing the gravity of the situation, Dan placed a quick phone call to Ian Morrison at his Lower Sackville home. Ian roused producer Mark Campbell, reporter Heather Proudfoot, a Pictou County native, and cameraman Jim Hill Jr., dispatching them to Plymouth with the suggestion that they pack an overnight bag.

Calls had quickly gone out to draeggermen, miners, and former miners trained in the risky techniques of mine rescue. Many came without being asked. It was several hours before I learned of the explosion and the monumental rescue effort that was being mounted. Turning on my television set around noon, I assumed the "powerful explosion" the CNN anchor was speaking of had occurred in Russia or China or somewhere far away, where it seemed such tragedies usually happened. I went numb in disbelief when a map of Nova Scotia appeared on the screen. It was the same sort of feeling I experienced five years later as

Lloyd Robertson reported the crash of a passenger aircraft off Peggy's Cove.

In each case, I immediately phoned the ATV newscentre to inquire about what I could do, then proceeded to get cleaned up, pack a suit, shirt, and tie into a garment bag, and head into the station. The newsroom seemed strangely silent early in the afternoon of May 9. Ian Morrison, John Soosaar, and weekend anchor/reporter Jonathan Gravenor were quietly working the phones. Campbell, Proudfoot, and several of our best technical people were already in Plymouth. ATV's mobile satellite truck had been diverted to Pictou County on its way back to Halifax from another community suffering in stunned disbelief. A few days earlier, three teenagers had been shot and killed during a robbery at the McDonald's restaurant in Sydney River. Another young woman lay seriously injured in hospital. Three teens were later charged and convicted of the crimes. Working in the newsroom on that Saturday afternoon, none of us could quite believe that for the second time in less than a week, a Nova Scotia tragedy was dominating world headlines.

As the afternoon wore on, Ian suggested I prepare to co-anchor a special report with Jonathan Gravenor. John Soosaar, who had spent his youth in Pictou County after immigrating to Canada from Estonia in the 1950s, had arranged for us to speak live with renowned local mining expert Bob Hoegg. Bob's expertise came from firsthand knowledge: he had worked and managed mines and by his own admission "had coal dust in his veins."

At shortly after 3:00 P.M. on May 9, 1992, just ten hours after the mine explosion, Bob Hoegg grimly confided the he did not hold out much hope that anyone had survived. As for the cause of the blast, he correctly theorized that coal dust had powered a methane gas explosion which, he pointed out, could have been ignited by the smallest spark. A man of considerable humility, Bob Hoegg quickly added that he might be wrong and sincerely hoped that he was.

As principal anchor of *The ATV Evening News*, Dave Wright

was the natural first choice to anchor our continuing coverage of the disaster and the rescue effort. Dave was at his cottage on the South Shore on that Saturday afternoon, and couldn't be reached, despite repeated attempts. Late in the afternoon, Ian Morrison suggested I travel to Plymouth with audio technician Grant Kennedy, who was being dispatched to deliver a station wagon full of equipment. Ian suggested that we might be needed to stay overnight. It was, in fact, several days before either of us returned to Halifax.

By the early evening of May 9, the tiny community centre in Plymouth was a beehive of media activity. Reporters, photographers, and technicians from several dozen news organizations had descended on the scene to cover the search for survivors. There had already been several regular media briefings given by RCMP constable Ivan Baker and the ultra slick Colin Benner, Curragh Resources's vice-president and spin doctor. ATV interrupted programming as events warranted, even remaining on the air overnight to provide information to thousands of viewers who by then were keeping a vigil. ATV technician Jeff Oakley was routinely originating satellite feeds to a host of world broadcasters. In the wee hours of Sunday morning, Mother's Day 1992, Mike Duffy arrived at Plymouth to host his flagship newsmagazine *Sunday Edition* live from the site. I joined Mike with updates on the latest developments in the search and rescue, as the broadcast went live into each of Canada's five major time zones. It was the first and perhaps only time there were five distinctive *Sunday Editions*. The public simply couldn't get enough information about the search for survivors. ATV and ASN were carrying frequent news updates and all of the stations' newscasts were originating in their entirety or in part from Plymouth. ASN anchor Ron Kronstein arrived on the site around the same time I did, and within hours, we were co-anchoring improvised news specials simulcast on the two stations.

Even the broadcasts that aired in the middle of those first few nights were widely watched, judging from the comments we received later. I developed a healthy respect for Ron's technical knowledge. He had worked in Sudbury, Ontario, and was familiar with both mining (albeit hard rock mining) and rescue techniques. He mastered the intricacies of Westray's layout and was able to explain the logistics and location of the rescue effort. I concentrated on covering the more emotional side of the story. The coverage was virtually non-stop: it was a good forty hours before any of us got any sleep.

During those first few days, there was little if any talk about criminality. The RCMP officers on the scene were essentially directing traffic to or away from the mine site and sheltering members of the miners' families, who had gathered at the fire hall just a short walk from the community centre. For once, those personally touched by a tragedy and most of those covering it were motivated by precisely the same emotion: hope. Among the journalists there was, at least in the early hours after the explosion, an informal understanding that the focus of the story was the rescue effort. There was a somewhat more formal agreement that no media person would attempt to violate the privacy of the families at the fire hall. A few of the relatives ventured over to speak with us, but such encounters were low key and usually off the record.

Back in Halifax, Rick Grant, working closely with John Soosaar, was already reporting on what appeared to be irregularities in the operation of the mine, particularly the inspection process. Many of those early stories also touched on the highly charged political climate in which the Westray project had been approved and developed. As the week wore on, the spark of hope flickered and media attention shifted from a story of rescue to a story of grief and blame. We returned to Halifax that Friday, after six physically and emotionally exhausting days spent mostly at the community centre, with perhaps eighteen hours of sleep at the Peter Pan Motel. We were back in Pictou County several days later for a memorial service attended by grieving families and friends from across the country. The Prime Minister was there, as was the premier and a host of other dignitaries. The service which was broadcast nationally brought a degree of closure for many of those who lost loved ones, some of them entombed in the devastated mine.

The Plymouth Community Centre was quiet and practically deserted on the summer Saturday afternoon when Ian Morrison, Ron Kronstein, Jeff Oakley, and I made our final visit. There we met briefly with members of the community, presenting them with a small token of thanks for their generosity and hospitality during the difficult days after the tragedy. They are some of the most remarkable people I have ever met.

The same courage and strength of character were in evidence six and a half years later when a Swissair jet crashed off the Nova Scotian coast. Fishermen from around St. Margaret's Bay immediately took to their boats, true to the time-honoured practice of offering assistance to others in trouble at sea. They went without encouragement, prowling the bay for signs of life, finding instead only signs of death and destruction.

Like Westray, the coverage of the crash of Swissair Flight 111 began as a story of hope. When ATV went to air at just before 12:30 A.M. on the morning of September 3, 1998, Halifax-area hospitals were on standby to receive survivors. At that early stage, we had no way of knowing that no one could possibly have survived the impact. But it wasn't long before that fact became all too apparent. A young reporter named Kim Brunhuber, who was working with us for the summer, reported by telephone that only relatively small pieces of debris and the contents of shattered suitcases were being recovered. There were no survivors, not even any bodies. We reported that grim news shortly after 3:00 A.M. to an audience around the world. Our broadcast was being carried on CNN and ABC and picked up by stations around the globe. I spoke with one person who watched the tragic story unfold in his Tokyo hotel room. Our news team stayed on the air all night, reporting in detail on what was by then a recovery effort. ATV sound engineer Grant Kennedy, who flew his small plane from Yarmouth to Shearwater just ahead of the doomed jet, told us about the sky and weather conditions. He observed that it was an extremely dark night; there was no moon and few reference points, even for a pilot familiar with the geography.

Residents of the area spoke with us on the telephone, detailing what they had seen and heard during and after the plane's final uncontrolled descent. Flight 111 was en route to Geneva and Zurich, Switzerland, from New York's Kennedy International Airport, when it encountered problems and declared a "pan pan pan" emergency off the coast of Nova Scotia. Captain Hans Zimmerman attempted to reach Halifax International Airport; people working at the airport that night told me they saw the lights of the troubled airliner. For whatever reason, the plane turned away from the airport and crashed a short time later. A large debris field was visible on the water and an impact point had been ascertained by the time we signed off our local broadcast at 7:30 A.M. CTV's Dan Matheson, who had arrived on the scene, then anchored *Canada AM* from windy and wet Peggy's Cove.

It was an international news story, and of particular interest and importance to the New York City media. It wasn't long before satellite trucks from the four major American networks and some large local affiliates were sprouting on the rocks near the famous Peggy's Cove lighthouse. The media circus lasted for a week, as the grieving relatives of the victims arrived, mostly from New York and Switzerland. The Red Cross provided counseling to the grief stricken and to those traumatized by the disturbing discoveries they had made on the water and along the shoreline after the crash.

A memorial service was attended by many of the victims' families, representatives of the Canadian, Swiss, and American governments, and clergy from several major religions. There is a monument to the victims of Swissair Flight 111, and the crash site itself is designated on marine charts as a memorial to all of those who lost their lives. Through it all, the citizens of Peggy's Cove and all of the villages of St. Margaret's Bay offered comfort and compassion in every way they could.

Volunteers shuttled the mourners to and from the crash site, many offered personal support and hospitality. The larger community of Nova Scotia honoured the families of the dead mostly by leaving them alone.

Eyewitness to History

HISTORY IS LIKELY TO RECALL the fall of the Berlin wall as one of the key events of the twentieth century. The wall, erected virtually overnight during the chilliest days of the cold war in the sixties, came down almost as quickly in the fall of 1989. Hundreds of millions of people on every continent and in every time zone witnessed it on live television. But viewers in the Maritime provinces had a unique vantage point—local perspective on a momentous international event.

Just how Dave Wright ended up standing there at the Brandenberg gate as the wall came down is a tale that involves almost equal measures of good, hard work and very good luck. The winds of change began blowing across Europe in April 1989, when the Solidarity trade union movement won the right to free elections in communist Poland. Two months later, Solidarity won control of the Polish government. That spark of democracy ignited a burning desire for freedom throughout Eastern Europe. In Hungary, the government responded by dismantling its border with Austria, allowing virtually free movement into the West; Czechoslovakia took no action against growing public demonstrations, and speculation that East

Germany was about to open the border in the divided city of Berlin mounted.

That was all Dave needed to hear. He quickly convinced Harris Sullivan and Dick Prat that ATV should be there to bring the story home to Maritimers. Dave, producer Mark Campbell, and cameraman Pat Kennedy hastily made their way to the former German capital, arriving just as the wall started to crumble at the hands of people with pickaxes. Mark had contacted his old friend and former colleague John Beatty at CJOH Television in Ottawa, suggesting the two stations share resources in covering the big story in Europe. Beatty, a master of organization and well known for his love of travel, agreed almost immediately, and the two news crews teamed up in Berlin. Mark and John arranged for facilities "on the ground," including a fantastic live location just metres from the Brandenberg gate. Eagle-eyed news junkies probably noticed that Dave Wright anchored *The ATV Evening News* from exactly the same location used by Tom Brokaw for *NBC Nightly News*. About a year later, Dave was back in Germany, reporting on how the changing political situation in Western Europe had precipitated the closure of Canadian Forces bases there.

Dave Wright and Mark Campbell did some of their best work in the field. Dave had a gift for finding local angles in international stories and a knack for telling them in a unique, homespun way. Mark also played a major role in a couple of historic *Live at 5* specials. In May of 1990, with the Iron Curtain in shreds, Soviet president Mikhail Gorbachev stopped in Ottawa en route to a meeting in Washington with President George Bush (the first). "Gorby" and his stylish wife Raisa had become real media stars, and Mark Campbell suggested their activities in Ottawa would make good *Live at 5* content. So off we flew to the nation's capital, just the two of us, planning to borrow technical facilities from our friends at CJOH. After managing to get media credentials, we proceeded to the Uplands Air Force base. It was secured like a prison under lockdown; after passing through not one but two metal detectors and a body search, we

DAVE WRIGHT REPORTS FROM
GERMANY on the changing political
climate in Europe and the closure of
Canadian bases in 1990.

were permitted onto the tarmac where our live broadcast location was set up on a small pedestal, a hundred metres from President Gorbachev's Aeroflot jet. I was joined for some of the broadcast by Mike Duffy, whose famous face got him through the security perimeter in a matter of seconds after he was held up in traffic. We signed off at five-thirty Atlantic time, in time for CTV coverage of a news conference by Gorbachev and Brian Mulroney. Mike, Mark, and I moved inside the huge hangar where the two leaders were to speak, joining a throng of reporters, photographers, police, and secret agents from Canada, the United States, and Russia. When the charismatic Gorabachev entered the room, Mark lifted a 35-millimetre camera to his eye to snap a photo of the political giant (who was actually a much shorter man than any of us expected). Before he could press the button to release the shutter, a large man barked in a heavily accented voice, "Take a picture of the floor." A perplexed Campbell grunted, "What?" The man, who was wearing the distinctive red-star of the KGB on his lapel, repeated "Take a picture of the floor." It was his way of making certain that it was really a camera, not a carefully concealed weapon that was pointed directly at his boss.

Six weeks later, Mark and I found ourselves on the road again, originating *Live at 5* from amid a crowd of six hundred thousand on the streets of Montreal. The occasion was the St. Jean Baptiste Day parade, always a big event in Montreal, although not always a national news event, as it was in June of 1990.

By a strange twist of history, the Meech Lake Constitutional Accord, conceived in secret by Brian Mulroney and the ten premiers in 1987, was pronounced officially dead the day before Quebec's national holiday. The deal called for a ratification vote by all provincial legislatures by June 23, 1990. Newfoundland premier Clyde Wells and Manitoba MLA Elijah Harper made sure that didn't happen. There was considerable disappointment and even anger in Quebec where the accord was widely seen as righting earlier constitutional wrongs. Many pundits expected obvious and emotional displays of Quebec nationalism, and

STEVE BROADCASTING VIA SATELLITE from the streets of Montreal following the collapse of the Meech Lake Accord. Hundreds of thousands turned out for the 1990 St-Jean-Baptiste Day parade.

some even feared violence during the St. Jean Baptiste Day parade the next day—but there was no parade the next day. Heavy rain forced organizers to postpone the parade for twenty-four hours, until Monday afternoon. Mark Campbell and I were having spaghetti and red wine with our future wives, Nicki Snowe and Jocelyn Corkum, when we learned of the postponement and realized the live TV opportunity it presented. The historic parade would be going on at five o'clock Atlantic time, and we could cover it live. We quickly worked through the logistics, taking full advantage of Jocelyn's technical acumen. As a director-producer, she knew what it would take to make it happen. With bare-bones details scribbled on a tomato-stained napkin, Mark and I placed a call to a skeptical Harris Sullivan. He was full of questions.

When would we leave? First thing in the morning.

Where would we stay? We wouldn't. We'd do the show and fly home.

Where would we work? Out of CTV affiliate CFCF.

Whose equipment would we use? We had no idea but Mark

ad-libbed that the CJOH Ottawa satellite truck would be available to us…which it was.

And the cost? Less than $1000…which it wasn't!

Probably as curious to see whether we could do it as he was supportive of trying, Harris gave the project the green light. Less than twelve hours later, Mark and I were in Montreal's Dorval airport, renting the cell phone that ate up our modest budget. We taxied into CFCF-TV and started working the phones. We devised several story ideas, Maritime angles on the collapse of the Meech Lake accord, which ATV reporters were working on. Back in Halifax, Jocelyn worked with technical supervisor Greg Campbell to set up satellite feeds from Montreal. We also arranged with Maritime Tel and Tel's Neil Sutherland for a *Live at 5* telephone poll on Clyde Wells' role in the collapse of the deal. On Clyde Wells, hero or villain? Maritimers overwhelmingly voted him a hero for sinking the deal.

Reporter Jonathan Gravenor used his contacts in Saskatchewan to secure an interview with Premier Grant Devine. John Buchanan agreed to appear on the programme, thereby allowing for a three-way conversation involving Halifax, Montreal, and Regina—ambitious TV for a project only hours in the making. In the end, it all went off (mostly) without a hitch, although Premier Devine was seen but never heard. No significant trouble hit Montreal that day, and the crowd for the parade was the largest in years. And Maritimers had a front row seat, *Live at 5*.

When Canada's East Coast navy was deployed as part of Operation Desert Storm, the international effort to contain Iraq, Dave immediately made plans to travel to the Middle East to report on Maritimers' roles there. Mark was just the sort of handler Dave needed to make technical arrangements, to get the material, edit it, and feed it back to Canada. Together, they sweet-talked and bribed their way into places they shouldn't have been. They got perilously close to the Iraqi border, where journalists in general and Western journalists in particular were considered hostile and therefore legitimate targets. They returned home unscathed, clutching receipts written in half a

[ABOVE] ATV'S LIVE BROADCAST of the departure of the Canadian fleet to the Persian Gulf on August 23, 1990. From left to right, Bill McKay, Dave Wright, and Steve Murphy.

ATV CAMERAMAN GREG IRVINE at the pyramids during coverage of the Canadian Navy's engagement in the Middle East.

dozen languages totaling many more Canadian dollars than Dick Prat had intended to spend. The trip to the Middle East was Dave's last major overseas shoot, although he and Campbell did travel to the Netherlands for a short series of stories about the smuggling of drugs and people into the Maritimes. And then, everything began to change.

Sign-offs

HARRIS SULLIVAN, WHO HAD BEEN ATV'S EDITORIAL COMPASS for a decade, surprised all of us by announcing his retirement in the spring of 1992. About a year earlier, Harris had been promoted to news director as part of a management restructuring that also saw Dick become the station's programme manager. Joe Irvine had moved to Halifax as vice-president and general manager after Marven Nathanson retired.

Management wasn't the only area getting a makeover. Dick Prat was already talking about and budgeting for a brand new home for ATV News. For the first time, he even had the space for the news complex he had always dreamed of. Radio stations CJCH and C100 were moving out of the television building into a stylish new facility with a fancy art deco design, the brainchild of Halifax developer Bob Stappells. That meant the ATV newsroom would be able to expand: outward, into the space vacated by the radio stations and the underutilized television production studio next door, and upward, into what Prat envisioned as a second storey of edit suites and offices tucked under the high studio ceilings. It was this ambitious vision of a snappy new newscentre that finally enticed Bill Patrick to move to Halifax.

"OUT WITH THE
OLD...."

Bill came to ATV from CHUM-owned CKVR in Barrie,
Ontario, but most of his considerable experience in television
had been in the much larger markets of Toronto and Detroit. In
fact, Patrick got in on the ground floor of what is widely considered to have been a television revolution: Moses Znaimer's
CITY-TV. The Toronto independent rewrote the book on how
local television shows are shot, edited, and produced. Bill started at CITY as a cameraman with another upstart named Stephen
Hurlbut, who is now vice-president of news for all of CHUM's
Toronto-area TV properties. Together they learned the art of
shooting pictures without tripods (the "shaky cam" to detrac-
tors of the style), without classic three-point lighting, and often
without reporters asking questions.

Bill rose through the ranks at CITY, with stints producing and
directing the flagship *CITY-Pulse at 6*, before eventually becoming Hurlbut's number two in the newsroom. He left the station,
apparently over budget issues, only to turn up a short time later
as executive producer at WDIV-TV, the hardboiled NBC affiliate in Detroit. He and his wife Nan moved to a suburb of the
motor (and murder) city, but returned to Barrie a couple of years

"…AND IN WITH THE NEW!" February 1993. ATV's new newscentre replaces the newsroom setting used since the mid-eighties.

later when things in Detroit soured.

Dick Prat had immense respect for Bill Patrick's programming skills and believed he was just the person to thoroughly modernize the image and style of ATV News. There hadn't been a significant change in its appearance since the debut of the last "new" newsroom, seven years earlier. In addition to the *Live at 5* refit, Bill Patrick was given a mandate to launch a new morning show on ASN. To produce the new *Breakfast Television*, he drafted Jocelyn Corkum, who was wrapping up production of CTV's *Wonder Why?* After several days of auditions, ASN news anchor Jill Krop (at that time, the real-life Mrs. Paul Mennier) was chosen as lead anchor for the new show, with a Toronto radio import named Mike Gligor as co-host. Finding a "third wheel," preferably a funnyman to host remote segments, proved more difficult. In a chance conversation with Jocelyn, Laura Lee Langley recommended she audition a Cape Breton radio personality and musician named Scott Boyd. Jocelyn and Bill knew instantly they had found their third host. Gligor didn't work out and was quickly replaced by veteran radio and television personality Kurt Stoodley. "BT" was an immediate hit,

branded by Fred Sherratt as the most successful morning show
ever launched in Canada.

After a couple of years, Jill returned to her native British
Columbia and was succeeded on "BT" by a multi-talented
woman Bill discovered at Halifax's Grafton Street Dinner theatre: Liz Rigney. Nine years later, Scott Boyd remains one of
Atlantic Canada's most popular television personalities. He
made the move to in-studio hosting in 1997 when Kurt Stoodley
was hired to anchor a newscast in Calgary. Over the years,
Scott's original role as "road warrior" was filled by three talented young men, two of whom came from the world of radio
and have since returned to it. Jay MacNeil was on the air in
Truro when he was tapped to co-host "BT." These days, he's a
big name in Toronto radio, where he's known as "the Maddog."
J.C. Douglas came to *Breakfast Television* from just across the
parking lot: Halifax rock station Q-104 is located in the CHUM
Radio building, which now houses the five-station Metro Radio
Group. J.C. returned to "Q" when he was offered the job of programme director. Jayson Baxter is a Lower Sackville Nova
Scotia native who was working in southern Ontario but anxious
to come home to Nova Scotia. He landed a job as a sports
reporter with ATV during the launch of CTV's *Sportsnet*, eventually making his way to the breakfast show by way of a stint
as a general assignment reporter with *The ATV Evening News*
and *Live at 5*. Liz Rigney's career has taken her in exactly the
opposite direction. The Charlottetown native traded her early
morning hosting duties for a supper-hour reporting job in
January 2002. Those who were surprised at the ease and com-
petence with which she made the move don't know the woman.
Liz has a degree in journalism from the University of King's
College hanging on the wall right beside her degree in music
from Mount Allison. She's a gifted musician and the only
reporter I know with two compact discs to her credit (although
ATV's Marc Patrone has one).

By his own admission, Bill Patrick is not a "big J" journalist.
But he is an acknowledged master of production style and technique. Bill arrived in Halifax with plans to oversee all style ele-

THE "BT" GANG:
Jill Krop, Scott
Boyd, and Kurt
Stoodley.

SCOTT BOYD HOLDS COURT at *Breakfast Television's*
first anniversary party. Fred Sherratt (right)
proclaimed "BT" the "most successful morning show
launch in Canadian history."

NEWS DIRECTOR
BILL PATRICK
brought major
market
experience to
ATV, with a
mandate
for change.

Liz Rigney was "discovered" by News Director Bill Patrick and Producer Jocelyn Murphy while she was singing for her supper at the Grafton Street Dinner Theatre, in Halifax.

ments of the "look" of the news stories, news programmes, and the news set (which in this case was to be the new newscentre). He appointed Mark Campbell senior producer of news, essentially the "keeper of the editorial flame."

It was Bill Patrick and Mark Campbell who established *Live at 5's* signature "First at 5" current affairs block. We had been featuring a story or two under the "First at 5" banner for several months before Bill's arrival, but it was his idea to make it the cornerstone of the show. He articulated that "First at 5" topics should be what everybody is talking about or what they will be talking about after seeing "First at 5." That definition pretty well holds to this day. The topics have ranged from the profound to the light-hearted but have usually been controversial or of very broad interest. Bill Patrick also invented what has grown into one of *Live at 5's* most popular and successful segments—"On Your Side." Yvonne Colbert resisted the assignment—that she champion good causes for those who couldn't get satisfaction for themselves—when she first heard about it, but went on to become a household name because of it. At the time, Yvonne was the highly regarded co-host of ASN's *Atlantic Pulse* news-

Yvonne Colbert was well respected as a news anchor on ASN, but became famous with "On Your Side."

cast with Ron Kronstein. Although not impressed with Patrick's suggestion that she become a supporting player on *Live at 5*, she grew to realize both the value of what she was doing and the profile it created for her.

Yvonne's first day of "On Your Side" was my last day as host of *Live at 5,* although I didn't know it at the time. It was February 1993, our first day on the air from the sparkling new newscentre. Hundreds of dignitaries and advertisers joined ATV's owners and senior managers for a party to celebrate the new facility. Broadcast from right in the middle of the festivities, *Live at 5* featured a story by Paul Mennier revealing how the place had been built over the preceding months. Nancy Regan took viewers on a tour, showing off all the new bells and whistles. Rita MacNeil dropped in for a feature interview, and when it was all over, Dave Wright anchored *The ATV Evening News* from a new desk at the front of the newsroom.

Immediately after the debut, Jocelyn and I left for Freeport, Bahamas, with my sister Ellen and her then husband. A few days later, we were married at Mary Star of the Sea Church where, by sheer and joyful coincidence, the parish priest was a Cape

Bretoner named Ambrose MacKinnon—a man as big-hearted as he is big! Returning to Halifax ten days later, a newly and happily married man, I never expected that my professional life was also about to undergo a major change.

Bill Patrick had already informed me of his plan to have me substitute on the evening news when Dave Wright was away, so I wasn't surprised when I was asked to fill in the day I got back. Dave was away—indefinitely—under somewhat mysterious circumstances. It turned out he was in Florida with Audrey, dealing with what was first described as "stress." Dave later told the Halifax *Chronicle-Herald* that he was suffering from clinical depression and was unable to continue anchoring *The ATV Evening News*. His decision to retire came as a shock to both his colleagues and his legion of viewers. For one thing, most people were surprised to learn that "Boomer" was old enough to retire. He had never spoken publicly about retiring, at least not seriously. But one night in March 1993, he appeared on *Live at 5* in a short segment taped in Miramichi, New Brunswick, to say thank you and good bye. It was Dave's last appearance on ATV.

Bill Patrick suggested I say a few words in tribute to the man who, more than anyone else, had become the physical embodiment of ATV News. I remember labouring for several hours over what I would say about my colleague, mentor, and friend. It's as true today as it was then:

I've always admired Dave Wright. First, as a viewer, a radio rookie, who thought his walking and talking style was just about the neatest thing on TV. I didn't realize until much later that he invented that style of TV. That's Dave the innovator.

When, a few years later I found myself working with Dave, I came to admire his generosity. Then, as now, he was quick to share his ideas, experiences, and considerable expertise with all of us. That's Dave the leader, the teacher, and storyteller.

We all admired Dave's decision to tackle one of North America's biggest TV markets at an age when many people are looking forward to smaller challenges. Like you, we missed him

"IT'S TRUE...THE MOST TRUSTED MAN IN THE MARITIMES, Dave Wright, has retired." On April 8, 1993, Bill Patrick announced Dave's sudden departure after "a trying time." Dave was suffering from clinical depression.

when he left, we worried when he suffered his heart attack, we rejoiced when he got better and came back. We've been worried about Dave lately; we hoped he'd get better and come back but we accept his decision that getting better means not coming back. We accept it because it's important to respect people you admire and we've always admired Dave.

The next day, for the third and final time, I was named to succeed Dave Wright.

A New Team

WITH MY MOVE TO *THE ATV EVENING NEWS* DESK in the spring of 1993, my old school friend Paul Mennier was appointed co-anchor of *Live at 5* with Nancy Regan. A few months later, meteorologist Richard Zurawski left the station over creative differences and was replaced by a young New Brunswicker fresh out of meteorology school. Steve Weagle's arrival on *Live at 5* capped a year of change even more pervasive than the 1988 exodus to MITV. In a relatively short period of time, two major personalities, Dave and Richard, left the show; Yvonne was added, Paul and I changed roles, and the set, logos, and shooting and editing styles were all updated. Not everyone approved of these changes—in fact, the critics were downright hostile about some of them. But in the spring of 1994, the people of the Maritime Provinces signaled their approval, handing *Live at 5* and *The ATV Evening News* a huge increase in ratings. The shows were drawing well in excess of a quarter of a million viewers a day.

Bill Patrick also put *Live at 5* on the road again, with an ambitious Florida "Spring Fling" that saw Paul and Nancy broadcasting live from five cities in five days. The shows followed a

THE NEW TEAM:
Steve Weagle,
Paul Mennier,
Steve Murphy,
Nancy Regan,
and Yvonne
Colbert.

"Celebrate the Maritimes" format, focusing on local attractions and people—treating viewers to a sort of vicarious winter vacation.

A year later, the news team produced some of the most memorable live event coverage in its history. The occasion was the G-7 Summit. The annual gathering of the leaders of the world's seven largest developed economies is like the Olympics of world politics. Many observers were shocked when Prime Minister Jean Chretien announced that Halifax, not Quebec City (as was widely expected), would host the 1995 G-7. The Nova Scotia capital was thought by some to be too small to accommodate seven presidential and prime ministerial delegations, and the thousands of media who cover their every move. Indeed, Halifax was the smallest world city ever to host a G-7 and doing so required some improvising. For one thing, since for security reasons only one leader was permitted to stay in each hotel, Halifax had just barely enough "presidential suites" to go around. Some of the journalists covering the summit were forced to stay well outside the city, prompting some grumbling from a few of them, accustomed as they were to the five-star

ATV's Starr Dobson reporting from the throng that came out to witness the 1995 G-7 Summit in Halifax.

treatment. There was also the question of where to hold the high-level meetings of the world leaders. Eventually, a squat waterfront building called Cornwallis Place (but known locally as "The Green Toad") was chosen as the location for the official part of the summit. It was the unofficial parts that turned downtown Halifax into a carnival. Summit organizers made good use of an abandoned lot on Barrington Street, building a temporary "International Café." There, locals and visitors alike came to sip the coffees, wines, and beers of the world. The café became a popular hangout before, during, and after the summit. An added advantage, of course, was that it camouflaged an otherwise ugly blemish on the urban landscape.

The partially completed hotel at the airport was another story. As visitors stepped out of the arrivals terminal, they were greeted by a grey-brown concrete "blob." Construction on the airport had halted when the owners ran out of money. Officials did the best they could to make it look like a "work in progress." A few cynics suggested hiring people to walk around in hard hats and t-shirts to make it look like it was still actually under construction. Of course the actual summiteers and their cronies never saw

JONATHAN KAY never did find NBC's Irving R. Levine, who criticized "small-town" Halifax during the G-7 Summit. (But Wolf Blizter did get a *Breakfast Television* mug from "BT" funnyman Mark Scholz.)

the hulking embarrassment; they all arrived at CFB Shearwater where everything was polished and shined in the best military tradition. Across the harbour in downtown Halifax, there was an orgy of paving and painting and potted plants. The old city looked as good as new when the first of the official delegations arrived.

ATV covered the summit like the world-class political and social event that it was. For the first and one of only a few times in history, *Live at 5* and *The ATV Evening News* were rolled into one programme, anchored by Paul, Nancy, and myself, entirely from in and around the Grand Parade square in Halifax. The CTV network had been chosen as host broadcaster for the 1995 G-7. It was up to CTV to provide video and audio coverage of every summit event to broadcasters from around the world. To do this, CTV cameras were granted privileged access to locations off-limits to other media. As a CTV affiliate, ATV had full use of the network pictures, in addition to shots from half a dozen of its own cameras. It all came together in three ninety-minute specials, one of which featured an impromptu "drive by" by Russian president Boris Yeltsin. A crowd favourite, President Yeltsin's overt antics also prompted speculation about his sobriety.

Bill and Hilary Clinton were unquestionably the biggest stars of the summit. President Clinton turned heads and drew cheers everywhere he went, while the First Lady was enthusiastically received at Mount St. Vincent University, which conferred upon her an honourary degree. Jean Chrétien, still basking in the glow of his 1993 election victory, was greeted with smiles and hand-shakes on his way to and from every event. In fact, spectators offered up applause and *oohs* and *ahs* for all of the world leaders, or at least the ones they recognized. German chancellor Helmut Kohl surprised downtown office workers, and probably panicked his security handlers, when he opted to walk down Lower Water Street to a morning meeting. Jacques Chirac was on one of his first foreign forays as French president and was not always instantly recognized by starwatchers. The prime ministers of Japan and Italy were applauded only after they stepped out of, or into, flag-bearing limousines. The secretary-general of the European Union drew perplexed stares and halting applause from people uncertain about who he was but confident he was probably somebody important. And yes, there were also a few people who were politely applauded by uncertain crowds even though they weren't "somebody important."

Several ATV reporters had encounters close up with world leaders; Rick Grant came face-to-face briefly with Bill Clinton. It was one of the few times in his life when Rick didn't get a chance to grill a politician within earshot about some controversy or scandal. Shaking the President's hand, Grant intended to fire off a question about Russian involvement in Chechnya but didn't get beyond, "Hello, Mr. President" before the leader of the free world was whisked away.

When all was said and done, everyone agreed Halifax had done a good job hosting the world. Well, almost everyone. Bow-tied NBC correspondent Irving R. Levine was clearly not impressed with the small city summit, and said so! ATV's Jonathan Kay was particularly offended by Levine's remarks, so he donned a bow-tie of his own and skulked around downtown Halifax, camera in tow, looking for the offender. Irving R. Levine wasn't available for an interview. Neither was CNN's Wolf Blitzer, arguably the

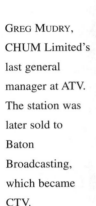

GREG MUDRY, CHUM Limited's last general manager at ATV. The station was later sold to Baton Broadcasting, which became CTV.

biggest media star to attend the summit.

Live at 5's ratings got better and better under Bill Patrick's leadership, but morale in the newsroom did not. Bill's constant drive for perfection had yielded a superlative product but had also intimidated many staff members, estranging a great many. After a tumultuous final six months, Bill accepted CHUM's invitation to return to the Barrie station, which was about to be reinvented in CITY-TV style. Mark Campbell took a producer's position in Toronto. The two left behind a legacy of greatly improved ratings and some spectacular programming accomplishments.

ATV vice-president and general manager Greg Mudry, who had come to Halifax the previous year when Joe Irvine retired, asked Dick Prat to reassume the news director's role on an acting basis while he searched for a permanent replacement for Patrick. Eventually, they settled on a fast-rising star from CBC Alberta named Bob McLaughlin. He was hired with a mandate to mend fences and "toughen up" the news, which some people felt had become too soft. To oversee the storytelling, Bob brought in Jay Witherbee, a promising young CBC producer with whom he had worked in Edmonton. Jay arrived in Halifax on the day of

TV ROOKIE
Ajantha
Jayabarathan,
a.k.a. "Dr. AJ."

the ATV Christmas party in December 1995, introducing himself to everyone as "the new guy."

It was under McLaughlin's leadership that producer Peter Hays, who had been hired away from the Halifax *Daily News,* lured greengrocer Pete Luckett into the *Live at 5* stable. Pete had become nationally famous on CBC television's *Midday* programme, offering up a weekly sampling of wit and wisdom about produce and life from his "Frootique" in the Saint John City Market. Somehow, McLaughlin and Hays made life appear "greener on the other side of the grocery aisle" (and the TV dial). Pairing Pete with Nancy Regan in segments produced at his Bedford location proved a masterstroke. The chemistry between them is remarkable and she is more than capable as a foil for his quick cockney wit!

Peter and Bob also brought Ajantha Jayabarathan on board. "Dr. A.J.," as she is better known to almost everyone (except her husband Dan, her son Kirk, daughter Onika, and the rest of her family), has built on a solid foundation of medical reporting laid by Dr. Stewart Cameron, who made *Live at 5* housecalls for almost a decade. Like Stewart, Dr. A.J. has a friendly

TV VETERAN
Stewart
Cameron. In the
eighties, he was
Live at 5's first
doctor. In the
seventies, he was
an ATV weather
anchor.

yet authoritative presence on television. Unlike Stewart, who
did some part-time work at ATV while he was going to university, AJ had no television experience before taking up the position. Today, after only a few years, she is a natural who could
easily have a career in television should she ever decide to hang
up her stethoscope.

Bob McLaughlin's initiatives brought further ratings
improvements, but his greatest impact was felt after he left ATV
to launch Baton Broadcasting's new television news operation
in Vancouver. Baton, the Toronto-based television-company
controlled by the Eaton family, acquired ATV from CHUM in
early 1997. The deal involved an asset swap that saw CHUM
take over Baton's TV stations in London, Pembroke, and
Wingham, Ontario, in exchange for the ATV stations in Halifax,
Moncton, Sydney, and Saint John, plus $10 million.

It was a transaction involving only medium- and small-mar-
ket television stations, but it had a major impact on the entire
Canadian broadcasting industry. That's because ATV's 14.3 per
cent share in CTV gave Baton Broadcasting 57 per cent ownership and effective control of the long-fractured network. Fred

THE NEWS SUMMIT. A rare gathering of the entire ATV news staff in Halifax in 1996.

Sherratt broke the news of the swap to the shocked staff of ATV at a hastily called meeting on February 25, 1997. The new arrangement made ATV a wholly "O&O" (owned and operated) station, and part of an eastern group of CTV stations under the leadership of broadcasting veteran George Lund. To run the new East Coast properties, Lund chose Mike Elgie, the young and successful vice-president and general manager of the Baton station in Sault Ste. Marie, Ontario. The incumbent general manager, Greg Mudry, was re-assigned to CFPL-TV in London, after an interim period of "due diligence" during which the CRTC reviewed and approved the transaction.

Bob McLaughlin, who was known to Baton CEO Ivan Fecan, was drafted to set up the newsroom at the newly licensed Vancouver Television. To anchor his flagship newscast, he wanted none other than Paul Mennier. Paul accepted the offer and rode off into the sunset—literally! He left the ATV parking lot on horseback in the late summer of 1997. By then, news director Jay Witherbee was dealing with a rash of staff defections to other, mostly new, television stations in Western Canada. Former ATV senior producer Mark Campbell had been hired

MIKE ELGIE. The young Sault Ste. Marie, Ontario, native was named vice-president and general manager of ATV by Baton Broadcasting (now CTV).

away from CITY-TV to launch news operations for the Craig family's new A-Channel stations in Alberta. He lured *Breakfast Television's* Kurt Stoodley to Calgary to anchor a supper-hour newsmagazine show modeled and named after *Live at 5*. The irrepressible Mark Scholz, a former "BT" guest host, got his own morning show, *The Big Breakfast*, on A-Channel Edmonton. ASN entertainment maven Joanne Nugent was hired to co-host an Edmonton edition of *Live at 5*.

Ironically, ATV ultimately looked west for Paul Mennier's replacement, but Ron Kronstein was familiar to Maritimers when he was chosen to become Nancy Regan's co-host in the spring of 1998. Ron spent more than a decade anchoring ASN's *Atlantic Pulse* newscasts before moving to Winnipeg's CTV affiliate CKY-5. In Winnipeg, Ron again distinguished himself with his live reports during the destructive floods that hit the city. But with strong family ties in the Maritimes (his son lives in the Halifax area and his in-laws are Cape Bretoners), Ron and his wife Michelle Gillis were anxious to return to the East Coast. The *Live at 5* opportunity made that possible.

Most of us expected Ron's return to signal the end of what

NANCY AND PAUL. Their five-year on-air partnership ended when Mennier moved to VTV. Paul had been on *Live at 5* for fourteen years.

seemed like a "cycle of change" being repeated every three of four years. But we were wrong. In the spring of 1998, Steve Weagle's dream of working in the United States came true when he landed a position in West Palm Beach, Florida, where he now tracks hurricanes and high-pressure areas as chief meteorologist at NBC affiliate WPTV. His spot on *Live at 5* and *The ATV Evening News* was quickly, and logically, filled by Peter Coade. who had been doing forecasts on *ATV News1* and the *ATV Weekend News* since the demise of ASN's *Atlantic Pulse*. Peter is a Halifax native (in fact he was born just a couple of blocks from ATV's Robie Street studios), who worked his way through the Weather Service, eventually becoming officer-in-charge at the flagship Toronto weather office. It was in that role that he became a media star, appearing regularly on Toronto's most prestigious private radio station, 1010 CFRB, home to such broadcasting luminaries as the late Gordon Sinclair, Betty Kennedy, and Wally Crouter. When ASN went looking for a media-experienced meteorologist for its primetime newscast in 1990, it furnished the perfect opportunity for Peter and Donna Coade to come home. Years later, restructuring saw *Atlantic*

A NEW BUT
FAMILIAR FACE.
Ron Kronstein
returned to the
Maritimes from
CKY Winnipeg
as co-host of
Live at 5.

Pulse replaced with a Headline News service, which did not require the services of a full-time meteorologist. Peter had in fact been given a layoff notice, as had co-anchor Cindy Burgess, when Steve Weagle announced his move to West Palm Beach.

Around that same time, Yvonne Colbert "crossed the street" and accepted an offer to join the CBC Halifax supper-hour programme as consumer reporter. Hiring one of *Live at 5's* most popular and competent performers was the brainchild of Mike Pietrus, CBC's shrewd and capable former executive producer. Pietrus was no stranger to Yvonne or to Halifax, having spent a couple of years toiling in the ATV newsroom in the early eighties. He had some inside knowledge of ATV, where the core philosophy hadn't changed much in the years since his departure. His strategy in hiring Yvonne was both simple and transparent: enhance his own programme while dealing a serious blow to ours. But it was only partly successful.

Yvonne Colbert's thorough and thoughtful reporting and friendly presentation would enhance any programme. Her departure was a loss to ATV and might have been a more serious blow were it not for Jay Witherbee's quick and inspired

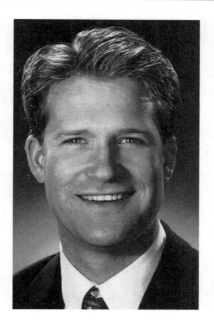

"WARMER WEATHER FROM THE WEST (AND SOUTH)." Steve Weagle's dream came true when he accepted a job at the NBC station in West Palm Beach, Florida.

decision to offer the "On Your Side" position to Starr Dobson. Starr's background made her well suited for the role of consumer advocate. From rural Nova Scotia like Yvonne (Yvonne is from Shelburne, while Starr is from Alma, Pictou County), she brings a certain small-town sensibility to her work. She is persistent without being overly aggressive, asking the tough questions without being "nasty." Starr became known to ATV viewers as Starr Cunningham, having joined ATV News as a general assignment reporter right out of the University of King's College School of Journalism. She was quickly accepted in her new role. Today, "On Your Side" generates more phone calls and mail than any other *Live at 5* segment, with the possible and occasional exception of the marriage "Milestones" and "Weather Watchers." Yvonne Colbert, who continued doing excellent consumer reporting for CBC, was a casualty in one of the interminable rounds of layoffs at the public broadcaster.

From the very beginning, *Live at 5* has covered entertainment stories, although in recent years the focus has sharpened on Maritime performers. Sydney's MairiAnna Bachynsky covers "The Scene" from Cape Breton to California. These days she's

PETER COADE
was a Toronto
radio star before
he returned home
to Halifax.

as likely to be chatting with Great Big Sea's Allan Doyle as she is sitting down with Mel Gibson in a posh Los Angeles hotel. It's a "scene" first staked out by Moncton-native Todd Battis, who returned home in the mid-nineties after several years with the CBC. In 2001, Todd traded entertainment for the environment: he's now CTV's Halifax-based oceans and climate specialist.

Live at 5 and its sister show, the expanded *ATV Evening News,* have remained largely unchanged through the late nineties and into the twenty-first century, despite consolidations at the local level and the veritable reconstruction of the Canadian broadcasting industry at the corporate level. Baton Broadcasting eventually reorganized and renamed itself CTV Television Inc., and was almost immediately acquired by Bell Canada Enterprises (BCE). The network and its stations, including ATV, are now part of an operating subsidiary called Bell-Globe Media, which also includes the *Globe and Mail* newspaper, and internet providers Lycos/Sympatico.

Even through the myriad of ownership changes, no attempt has ever been made to manipulate the style or content of *Live at Five* or *The ATV Evening News.* In fact, when ATV was

Starr Dobson,
"On Your Side."

Nancy with
MairiAnna
Bachynsky, live
in the control
room with "On
the Scene."

acquired by Baton, the new proprietors were quick to stipulate that they did not want to see any changes in the news product. Later, as president and CEO of the successor company, Ivan Fecan himself asserted his commitment to *Live at 5*, and held up ATV's regional approach to news coverage and broadcasting as an operating model for CTV stations.

The local editorial independence that CTV affords its owned and operated stations continues an approach begun by ATV's original out of province owners, CHUM Limited. Controlled by Ontario's Waters family, CHUM Limited devolved virtually all day-to-day management to the local level, where local people were firmly in control. With the growing concentration of media ownership in Canada, concerns about the narrowing of editorial control over the nation's news may be legitimate. But throughout its thirty-year history, ATV has always been owned by large Toronto corporations, not one of which has ever imprinted an editorial agenda on any news programme I have worked on. Perhaps that is why through all of the changes in ownership, *Live at 5* and *The ATV Evening News* have remained the most popular programmes on Maritime television.

Nine to Five

EVERY SO OFTEN, SOMEONE ASKS WHAT TIME MY DAY STARTS. Many people are genuinely surprised by the answer. The assumption seems to be that people who appear on television show up just in time to be handed a script, put on some make-up, and step in front of the camera. Oh, that it was so! Such assumptions are part of the over-arching optical illusion that is television. Well-produced TV shows are smoothly executed and appear unrehearsed, even spontaneous. In truth, a great deal of preparation goes into the spontaneity, and there's often near panic behind the smooth on-air facade!

Winnipeg-born Monty Hall is regarded as one of the smoothest television hosts in history. For years, he presided over "the marketplace of America" on ABC's *Let's Make A Deal,* a hugely successful (if quirky) game show in which Hall and his accomplice Jay Stewart bartered with costumed members of the studio audience for prizes hidden under boxes and behind curtains. Besides duping or "zonking" his contestants, Hall was also fond of offering cash for the most unlikely of items in a person's purse or wallet ("I'll give you $100 for an unpaid utility bill, $200 if it's two weeks overdue"). It all

seemed very unpredictable and unrehearsed, and Hall was considered an ad lib master, when in fact, he and his partner, producer Stefan Hatos, were master planners who anticipated and
scripted for virtually every possible outcome. Very little was left
to happenstance. Such is the grand illusion of television.

Live at 5 may look and feel like a friendly little get-together
that simply happens at five o'clock every day, but every programme represents a full day's work for dozens of people. It is
carefully and thoughtfully crafted by a team of producers that
often spends days or even weeks planning and putting together
a segment or story.

At ATV, most of the people who prepare the supper hour (the
two hours of *Live at 5* and *The ATV Evening News*) arrive at the
television station by nine o'clock in the morning. By then, a
blueprint for the day's *Live at 5* is already on the drawing board.
Columns or regular features are the backbone of *Live at 5*. Dr.
A.J.'s "House Calls," "Pete's Frootique," MairiAnna
Bachynsky's "The Scene," and even Starr Dobson's "On Your
Side" are often produced ahead of time. That's possible because
the subject matter has a shelf life of more than a day or two. But
the most critical component of *Live at 5* —"First at 5"—can't
be planned ahead. Deciding the focus for the topical and usually news-driven current affairs block that opens the show daily
is one of the most important decisions made during a meeting
that begins at 9:00 A.M. every day. The same session determines
which news stories are going to be covered by ATV reporters
across the region.

ATV's assignment editors, producers, anchors, and reporters
are expected to bring story ideas to the morning meeting, then
aggressively "pitch" or sell the stories they would like to do.
From this supermarket of ideas will often emerge a topic of suf-
ficient interest to warrant being "first at five" or the lead story
on *The ATV Evening News* at six o'clock. Viewers and others
often ask what we see as the difference between ATV's first
hour, *Live at 5,* and the second hour. Over the years several dis-
tinctions have emerged. First and foremost, as a newsmagazine
(a programme that contains many "departments," like a tradi-

WELCOME TO *LIVE AT 5*. Left to right, MairiAnna Bachynsky, Nancy Regan, Ron Kronstein, Starr Dobson, and Peter Coade.

tional general interest magazine) *Live at 5's* content is flexible. The show is able to be serious or light-hearted, as developments warrant. "First at Five" is designed to deal with the major issue of the day or the impact of the day's events. On a good day, the segment taps the first currents of public opinion. *The ATV Evening News,* by contrast, is a newscast of record, driven by events.

Recognizing important events is easier than sensing emerging public issues, although the two are often symbiotic. That's why the selection of the "First at Five" topic is so important. At the nine o'clock meeting, a great deal of time is spent debating the merits of several topics before settling on what will be on "First at Five." Then comes the equally tricky matter of how to tackle an issue. More often than not, there are three stories in the first block, each dealing with a particular angle on a single subject. Finding the clear and distinct "focus" for these stories is important but can be time consuming. When the process works as it should, "First at Five" is about what viewers are talking or thinking about by suppertime, or what they will be talking or thinking about after it.

Most days, about twenty people take part in the morning meeting, roughly half in person and the other half by conference call from ATV's newsrooms in Sydney, New Glasgow, Charlottetown, Moncton, Fredericton, and Saint John. The meeting begins with assignment editor Andy Leblanc calling for "breaking stories"—events already taking place or scheduled ahead of time. Quite often, reporters are already out of the newsrooms working on breaking stories before the meeting begins.

After nailing down what we call the "must-covers," the conversation immediately shifts to "First at Five." Sometimes the choice of topic is obvious. When the entire region or nation is fixated on a person, an event, or both (Sale and Pelletier or the hockey gold medals at the 2002 Olympics, for example), that's what's going to be first at five. On the days when the choice is not immediately apparent, producer Heather Macaulay usually offers up a topic or two already in development to start the discussion. Ron Kronstein and senior producer Wade Keller usually have suggestions. Somehow, after fifteen to thirty minutes of sometimes spirited discussion, a consensus forms about "First at Five." Reporters are then assigned their story lines and begin lining up the interviews and other material they will need to flesh out their supper hour reports. Through the day, reporters stay in close contact with Heather, who produces and writes "First at Five" and assists with the production of graphics or technical elements needed to round out the stories.

Good journalists always have good story ideas but they don't just make them up! Sure, lots of stories are born when a sharp eyed reporter notices something interesting or unusual, then allows her or his natural curiosity to take over. But good reporters also realize the golden rule at ATV News: every time the phone rings there's a chance it's a story. It might be a public relations person calling to promote something on behalf of a client, but just as likely, it's a viewer calling to tell us something they have seen or heard, something they believe should be on the news. Viewer calls fall into one of three categories: traditional news tips ("There's a fire next door..."), confidential insider information, or anecdotes about a family member, friend or neighbour. Many of these calls blossom into news stories. In the digital age, e-mail has become a vital source of information, but of course, some stories still arrive in the postal carrier's bag (around here, it all comes through Patrick Dunne, our intrepid shipper and receiver, who still processes hundreds of thousands of pieces of mail every year).

The point is, television news in general, and *Live at 5* in particular, is interactive. What we put on the air is often the direct result of what our viewers share with us, in person, in writing, or on the phone. That's not to say that every story we hear about will end up on the air. We receive hundreds of tips and suggestions every day and are able to broadcast only thirty or forty. Deciding which stories get on the air is the most difficult decision we make.

All of the *Live at 5* regulars (or irregulars, in the case of Pete Luckett!) have scheduled appearances on the programme. "On Your Side" and "The Scene" are daily features; Dr. A.J., Pete Luckett, and "Mrs. Fixit" are on two to four times per week. Dr. A.J. works closely with producer Dawn Veinotte, shooting material a few days ahead of time. Nancy Regan assumes responsibility for the production of "Pete's Frootique" segments of which she is a part, although she's quick to point out that she bears no responsibility for what Pete says. "Mrs. Fixit" (Rochester, New York's Terry McGrath) is a "hired hand" whose material comes in on tape through a news service.

Deciding the order in which all of these items appear is the job of Ron Kronstein, who, like every one of us who has hosted the programme, is also its lineup producer and head writer. This system flies in the face of the once popular assumptions about news anchors, rooted perhaps in *The Mary Tyler Moore Show*, in which Ted Baxter really did show up just in time to be handed a script, put on some makeup, and step in front of the camera!

At CBC, union and corporate practices are more restrictive. Although today, CBC's on-air presenters are in no way excluded from journalism as they were in 1976, when Lloyd Robertson quit CBC for CTV largely because as anchor he was not allowed to be involved in the news gathering, reporting, and writing.

The reality in local television in Canada is that almost every on-air personality has significant off-air duties. Some are managing editors who have final say on everything they read and a huge amount of influence over what gets covered and how.

At ATV almost everyone on the news staff performs several functions. Many of our reporters are weekend or substitute anchors; others shoot and edit their own material as videographers. Our producers, directors, and production assistants are also writers who assist reporters in the development of their stories as the news day unfolds.

Ron Kronstein has sketched the first "lineup" for *Live at 5* by about eleven o'clock in the morning but at that early hour nothing is etched in stone. Every so often, the best-laid editorial plans are overtaken by the events of the day. A story that looks like a sure thing at nine o'clock in the morning, sometimes doesn't make to air at all by five or six o'clock. When a major event transpires in the middle of the day or even later, *Live at 5* will re-jig its lineup to provide as much coverage as possible. The most difficult or controversial programming decisions are mediated by Wade Keller in his role as producer of the two hour slot, or by news director Jay Witherbee, whose approach is to encourage decision-making by consensus. Rarely is the entire two hours given over to a single event, as it was on September 11, 2001.

On a typical day, the look of *Live at 5* becomes clear by early afternoon. Heather Macaulay is fine-tuning the "First at Five" block, and Ron is massaging the lineup, deleting items and adding others, writing the continuity (the script) for the remainder of the programme, and planning special projects. *Live at 5* always has something special on the air or in the works: photo contests, health promotions, or giveaways. The technical producer and his control room and studio staff begin their day at 3:15 P.M., which may sound like plenty of time before the show starts at five o'clock, but it's always busy. There are segments to pre-tape, including a raft of promos (announcements that promote what's "coming up" on tomorrow's news programmes) and, frequently, interviews for the evening news. By 4:00, all of the *Live at 5* content has been "vetted" or approved by Heather, Ron, or another producer. Director Jocelyn Murphy is well into technical preparations, arranging for particular camera shots and graphics, and working with the technical staff on live feeds and any special requirements for the day's programme. Ron and Nancy spend the final hour before the programme reviewing scripts and recording promos.

What about makeup? Yes, we all wear it (in varying amounts) and no, there's no makeup artist—we apply it ourselves (with varying degrees of expertise).

Viewers get their first taste of what they can expect to see on the day's news programmes during a two-minute preview, which airs at roughly 4:40 during *The Oprah Winfrey Show*. Minutes later, as the second hand on the large clock in the ATV newsroom sweeps past five o'clock, the familiar theme music swells and *Live at 5* comes to life, as it has almost every weekday since 1982.

"Good evening and welcome to *Live at 5*… ."

Before the hour is over, viewers will experience an odyssey, through the important and the interesting, the topical and the trivial; news about themselves, their health, their lives, their community.

On the other side of the TV set, it's often a frantic sixty minutes of near misses. Stories that aren't quite ready when they're supposed to be, cameras whipping up narrow aisles at speeds exceeding the posted limits, technical glitches, large and small, and the most critical element in live television: the completely unexpected. Which answers two other questions we've all been asked: is it really live and what time is it on? Now you know we really are live at five.

Cast & Crew

THE SAYING THAT THINGS ARE NOT ALWAYS AS THEY APPEAR is particularly true of television. Viewers usually only see those of us who appear on camera. As a result, we tend to get more recognition than we deserve; more credit for things that go right, and, less often, more blame for things that go wrong. It's an extremely distorted view; just consider the math. For every one news anchor on camera, dozens of reporters, producers, directors, production assistants, floor directors, switchers, audio technicians, editors, and camera people are at work on the other side. And that doesn't include management, administrative and technical staff members, and marketing and sales people who, although not directly involved in a given production, are essential to keeping the television station operational. Over almost two decades, literally hundreds of people, most of whose names and faces are not instantly recognized, have played an essential role in the success of *ATV Evening News* and *Live at 5*. Others, you will likely remember, and some are household names.

Bill Jessome is one of the giants of Maritime broadcasting. The very personification of CJCB-TV in Sydney in the 1960s and 70s, hosting chat shows, the news, and performing live commercials, Bill returned to Cape Breton after working in the United States during the golden age of television. You can still catch his cameos on reruns of classic shows like *Gunsmoke* and *Route 66*. He also worked for the legendary Steve Allen at WMTW in Poland Springs, Maine.

Bill anchored the Sydney news during the days of Dave Wright's *Notebook*, occasionally hosting the five-thirty show when Dave was away. He became a news reporter when ATV went to its regional news format and eventually relocated to Halifax where he excelled in his coverage of the courts. Bill had a special way with judges, lawyers, and even suspects, who wouldn't talk to anyone else. But Bill's enduring claim to fame on *Live at 5,* and the stories for which he has become best known are the "Maritime Mysteries." Originally conceived as a local answer to NBC's *Unsolved Mysteries* series, Bill decided to focus almost exclusively on the paranormal. With master cameraman Kevin MacDonald behind the lens, the team recreated some of the most haunting chapters of Maritime history. Bill's meticulous research and his gravelly baritone delivery made for narratives that were one part history lesson, one part campfire ghost story. Kevin's brilliant staging, lighting, shooting and editing made for beautiful television. Following his "retirement," Bill published two delightful collections of *Maritime Mysteries*. (Don't read them alone!) Kevin MacDonald was a gifted artist whose camera work was recognized with several regional and national awards; he set the standard by which most ATV camera operators judge themselves. His life and career were cruelly cut short by cancer and we miss him. Kevin's widow, former ATV personality Debi Forsyth-Smith, and their children remain a part of our extended ATV family.

Blaine Henshaw and Ian Morrison were the two senior members of ATV's Halifax reporting team before and after *Live at 5's* 1982 sign-on. Henshaw was famous on the south shore of Nova Scotia, both as a radio personality and a musician, before joining ATV news in the 1970s. He also is a world-class auc-

BILL JESSOME—a giant in Maritime broadcasting.

tioneer and calls an ox pull better than just about anybody else. In the early eighties, Henshaw was ATV's lead reporter on the so-called "Roland Thornhill Affair," in which it was alleged that the Nova Scotia cabinet minister had received preferential treatment from the chartered banks in the settlement of his personal debts. These days, Blaine is a senior public affairs executive with the Nova Scotia government.

Ian Morrison had returned to the media after a stint in the Nova Scotia government with Gerald Regan's Liberals and, briefly, with the John Buchanan Progressive Conservatives. Morrison was a radio veteran who worked at CHNS in Halifax before joining the government. He covered everything but politics for ATV in the early eighties, and eventually rose through the newsroom ranks to the position of executive producer in the nineties. Along the way, he launched the news service (*Atlantic Pulse*) on ASN as senior producer and field produced most of the "Celebrate the Maritimes" programmes. He also oversaw ATV's election-night coverage, the newsroom's business affairs, and the installation of its first, second, and third newsroom computer systems. But to a great many people, he will always be Scrooge—the cranky character on the "Christmas Daddies" telecast played by Ian Morrison for almost twenty years.

Richard John "Rick" Grant has probably covered more stories in more cities than any other ATV reporter. I first met Rick in the late seventies when he was assigned to the ATV Saint John bureau. Part of his duties at that time included reading the western New Brunswick newscast which was inserted into Dave Wright's *Notebook*. The news was delivered from a desk in a ramshackle studio, with a floor so uneven the ATV logo on the wall was deliberately hung crooked so it would look straight to viewers at home!

The same logo, which was attached with two-sided tape, actually came unstuck one night and swung like a pendulum for several seconds while Rick read the news. That might have been all the convincing Rick needed that he'd rather report from the field than anchor from the studio, although he has continued to dabble in the latter. Rick is widely known as a reporter who "breaks" stories. He has done so as a political reporter at the legislatures in both Halifax and Fredericton, and on general assignment in St. John's and Halifax. As ASN's Newfoundland bureau chief, he was one of the first journalists on the scene after the Arrow Air DC-8, chartered to the U.S. military, crashed in Gander on December 12, 1985. 248 military personnel and eight crewmembers were killed in an accident officially blamed on aircraft icing, although years later many people insist it was an act of sabotage. Rick Grant filed some of the earliest reports about the crash and its cause. He also broke many of the early details following the 1992 Westray mine disaster and the crash of Swissair Flight 111 in 1998. Most of the really detailed television reporting on the burgeoning offshore oil and gas industry and the moribund shipbuilding industry has been done by Rick Grant.

The Hollingsworth name is synonymous with the media business in the Maritimes. Al Hollingsworth wrote a popular column, "The Morning After," in the Halifax *Daily News,* among other newspapers. He also edited the Kings County

TELEVISION CRAFTSMAN, the late
Kevin MacDonald. Among ATV
camermen, he is known as "The
King."

(New Brunswick) *Record*, and hosted a popular traditional country music show on Halifax radio station CHFX-FM, when he wasn't dabbling in Liberal Party politics, which he has done for decades. These days, another Hollingsworth is an up-and-coming member of the ATV News staff; he just happens to be the son of Al and Sharon Hollingsworth.

Paul Hollingsworth is another example of someone who was in the right place when opportunity came knocking. After completing a degree in journalism at the University of King's College, Paul signed on for part-time work as an autocue operator in the ATV newsroom. He came in early, stayed late, and otherwise volunteered his way into a job reading sports at night and on weekends. These days, he's a general assignment reporter who specializes in sports stories. He also turns up regularly on TSN and as a substitute anchor on ATV News programmes.

Heather Proudfoot joined ATV in Saint John in the early eighties after graduating from Ottawa's Carleton University School of Journalism. She later moved to Halifax and became a mainstay on *Live at 5* and *The ATV Evening News*. A real rarity in the television news business, Heather is a reporter equally comfortable unraveling a complex news story as spinning a human-interest feature. Heather's work is widely respected and although she is far too modest to admit it, she has declined lucrative opportunities to move to other stations in larger television markets, choosing instead to remain close to her family home in Pictou County.

Dartmouth native Jennifer Henderson worked with Heather in ATV's Saint John newsroom in the early eighties, and they remain close friends. A thorough and enterprising reporter, Jennifer has had several stints with ATV in Halifax over the years. These days, she reports on Maritime business issues for CBC Radio.

Bill McKay was ATV's long-time late-night anchor and a frequent stand-in for Dave Wright in the early days of *The Notebook* and later *Live at 5*. He co-hosted with Colleen Walsh the broadcast that began as *ATV News1* and continues today as *ATV News at Noon*. The Montreal native continues to reside in the Halifax area, toiling in the insurance industry. Colleen Walsh turns up from time to time on *CTV Newsnet*, after a successful career anchoring news for Global television in Toronto and a brief sojourn in the public affairs arena with Frank Stronach's Magna International.

Phonse Jessome spent a couple of years behind the *ATV News1* anchor desk, after a long and distinguished career reporting for ATV News in his native Cape Breton, New Glasgow, and Halifax. He also worked as a producer on *The ATV Evening News* before leaving the station to write books and work for the competition. He went over to "the dark side" to work for a brief time as a communications officer for the Sydney Tar Ponds cleanup.

John Waterman has done it all. The man who now anchors the morning updates on *Breakfast Television* cut his teeth in broadcasting in his native Annapolis Valley and at CFNB Fredericton, before joining CJCH Radio in 1972. He moved to ATV with Dick Prat and, but for a brief stint as an Air Canada flight attendant, has been with the station ever since. John was

IAN MORRISON'S ALTER-EGO,
Christmas Daddies' "Scrooge."

a general assignment reporter for years before carving out at a niche as *Live at 5's* first medical reporter. So credible and authoritative was he in that role that we privately (and jokingly) began referring to him as Dr. John. One night while introducing one of his reports I unintentionally identified him as "Dr. John" on the air—later clarifying that he only played a doctor on TV. John anchored the *ATV Late News* for several years, the morning news for several more, and has substituted on virtually every other ATV news programme.

The "late news" isn't so late anymore. The move of Lloyd Robertson's flagship CTV News from midnight to 11:00 P.M. in September 1998 saw the launch of "ATV News Nightside" at the more viewer-friendly hour of eleven-thirty. To anchor the programme, Jay Witherbee chose Saskatchewan native Bruce Frisko. Bruce came to Halifax to co-anchor ASN's *Atlantic Pulse* with Cindy Burgess after Ron Kronstein moved to CKY Winnipeg. In addition to his "Nightside" duties, Bruce now substitutes for Ron and myself on *Live at 5* and *The ATV Evening News* at six.

Prince Edward Island native Julie Caswell joined *ATV Headline News* after the Irvings sold their Saint John television station to the CBC. She's now a senior member of the Halifax newstaff.

Peter Mallette is still well remembered in northern Ontario, where he was the popular anchor of CTV's local news in Sudbury. These days, he is co-anchor of the ATV weekend news.

Elizabeth Chiu first came to the Maritimes in CTV's Atlantic news bureau, field producing for national reporter (and Bathurst native) Jim Munson, video editor Charlie Macdonald, and veteran cameraman Gord Danielson. Elizabeth polished her reporting skills at CTV's Parliament Hill bureau, before turning her talents to anchoring. Both Peter and Elizabeth are also senior members of the reporting team.

Like Starr Dobson, Jonathan Kay and Janice Landry joined ATV News straight out of journalism school as general assignment reporters. Each quickly became a valued member of the news team, and proved popular with viewers, particularly in their hometowns of Stellarton and Dartmouth. Over the years, Jonathan Kay also developed a reputation as one of ATV's most versatile storytellers. His reports always included animated "standups" (the part of a news story when the reporter is standing in front of the camera explaining a point), that were seldom standing still. He also authored three of ATV's most memorable April 1 stories. The first detailed champion pumpkin-grower Howard Dill's successful foray into giant carrots; another was about a giant iceberg in Halifax Harbour; and a third detailed ATV's move into 3-D broadcasting and the station's plan to send everyone in the Maritimes a pair of 3-D glasses. So convincing were these stories that officials from the Nova Scotia Department of Agriculture are said to have actually arrived at Dill's Windsor farm to examine the carrot. Unsuspecting curiosity seekers flocked from all over the Maritimes to witness the harbour iceberg and we still get the odd call from viewers wondering why they never received their 3-D glasses. Jonathan moved to the other side of the camera in 1999, briefly producing the *ATV Evening News at 6* before being snagged by *CTV Newsnet* in Toronto, where he is now a producer.

REPORTER RICK GRANT, with one of the handful of awards he has won during more than twenty years with ATV News.

Janice Landry made her mark as the station's crime reporter, and frequently substituted for Nancy Regan co-hosting *Live at 5*. She co-anchored the *ATV Weekend News* for several years with ATV's "other" Jonathan, Victoria-born Jonathan Gravenor, who came to the East Coast in the 1980s as a reporter in the Fredericton legislature news bureau. After moving to Halifax as an anchor and senior reporter, Jonathan jumped to "the network" as CTV's bureau chief in Winnipeg. Today he files reports from across Australia and New Zealand as the network's man down under.

Connell Smith and Sally Cummings were regular and popular contributors to *Live at 5* and *The ATV Evening News* before leaving ATV for other opportunities. Connell can be heard on CBC Radio's Saint John morning show, where he's also a producer. Sally now toils for the city of Saint John's Visitor and Convention Bureau.

Laverne Stewart and Kate Letterick, both of whom joined ATV right out of college, are still reporting, albeit in other media. Laverne writes for *The Gleaner* in Fredericton, and after flirting with politics and public relations, Kate signed on at CBC Radio in her hometown of Moncton.

VERSATILE REPORTER Heather
Proudfoot.

Another Monctonian, Greg Dennis, reported for ATV in
New Brunswick and Nova Scotia and is now a producer with
Global Television in Toronto. Wade Wilson, who was both a
news reporter and sportscaster in Moncton, turns up these days
in ATV news stories as a spokesperson for the New Brunswick
Department of Natural Resources. It's the same story with
Cape Breton's Greg Boone—after many years in the ATV
Cape Breton newsroom, he's now on camera speaking for the
Cape Breton Regional Hospital.

Halifax native Robert Rankin first established himself as a
solid and effective member of the ATV news team as a reporter
in Moncton before being assigned to the Halifax newsroom.
After a couple of years at Province House, covering the middle years of the John Buchanan government, he developed an
excellent reputation as the station's military reporter. Bob
toiled at CBC and CBC Newsworld before rejoining his long-
time friend Glen Carter at Calgary. Glen, the son of
Newfoundland politician Walter Carter, reported and anchored
for ATV and CJOH Ottawa; he now occupies the anchor chair
on the six o'clock news on "The A-Channel." Bob Rankin sits
in the producer's chair.

Allan MacLellan has had several careers at ATV Moncton,
including stints as a reporter and programme host, and lately
as a commercial producer. He remains well known across New

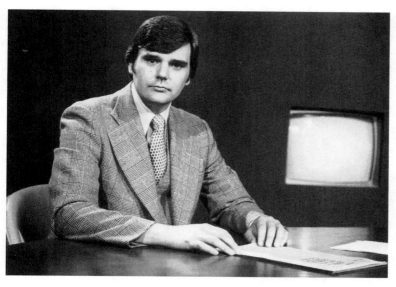

BILL MCKAY ON THE NEWS SET of the 1970s during his first "tour of duty" at ATV. He returned to the station in the eighties.

Brunswick as host of the "Christmas Daddies Telethon"; he is one of the driving forces behind the programme.

Mike Cameron, Ron Shaw, and Alex Vass remain the senior members of ATV's New Brunswick reporting staff. Mike joined ATV in 1984 as a reporter in Sydney, but he's been a cornerstone of the Saint John newsroom since the late eighties. With his sound editorial judgement and wry sense of humour, Mike has won legions of fans among his colleagues and viewers. Ron's mellifluous tones were familiar to listeners of CHSJ radio and television in Saint John for several years in the late seventies and early eighties. Alex started out in Port Hawkesbury in the early days of upstart radio station CIGO but was working on CFCY Charlottetown when he was hired for ATV's PEI bureau. He later moved to the Moncton station.

Saint John natives Paul Greene and Bruce Nesbit returned from points west to join ATV News to mind the store in Fredericton. MairiAnna Bachynksy and Jacqueline Foster, two young Nova Scotians who grew up watching ATV News in Sydney and Bridgetown, are now members of our news team.

Pictou County's Margaret McGee joined ATV News during Bob McLaughlin's tenure as news director, only to leave and

REPORTER AND AUTHOR Phonse
Jessome.

return again. Margaret came from and returned to CBC Radio,
where she broke stories and won awards for the Halifax
Information Morning programme. Now a freelance public
relations consultant, Maggie briefly rejoined the CTV family
as a correspondent in the Atlantic bureau, which is now con-
veniently and logically located down the hall from the ATV
Newscentre.

Until ATV's acquisition by CTV, the network's news staff
worked out of an office in downtown Halifax. Over the years,
some of Canada's best television journalists have worked out
of CTV's Atlantic bureau; many have gone on to distinguished
and seniors positions in broadcasting. Kevin Newman hosted
Good Morning America and substituted for Peter Jennings at
ABC before returning to Canada to work for CanWest Global.
Robert Hurst is now CTV's vice-president and general manager on the West Coast and Tom Walters is running his newsroom at CTV-BC. When not playing hockey or golf, Jim
Munson covered Parliament Hill for CTV. Del Archer rose
through the ranks at CTV News, eventually becoming vice-
president of news at CFCN Calgary. Del's ties to ATV are also
personal. His charming wife Cynthia Gregg, daughter of the

JOHN WATERMAN, with Dave Wright on the *I-D* set in the late seventies. In his thirty years on the air at ATV, John has done it all.

famous New Brunswick journalist Paddy, was a producer/director in the early days of the regional ATV News. Del and Cindy, as she's known to us, have recently resettled in Nova Scotia. No one at ATV is happier to have them back than Christina (Osmond) Holtorf, who joined the ATV newsroom from CHNS radio in the late seventies as a newsreader and reporter working with Cindy. They became and remain good friends. These days, Christina works on the assignment desk, juggling cameras (and the people who operate them), faxes, and telephones.

Kristen Tynes was a successful CBC Radio journalist when she decided to try her hand at television. After completing a masters in history at the University of Toronto, she returned to the newsroom as a producer on the *ATV Evening News at 6*. Kris has since returned to the classroom, as a high school history and English teacher in her hometown of Dartmouth.

Vancouver's Anne Drewa was working in Red Deer, Alberta, when she was spotted by Jay Witherbee and hired for a summer relief position. She's now a general reporter in Halifax.

Saskatchewan native Lane Farguson was the latest in a long line of keen, young journalists to cover the area from

JONATHAN
GRAVENOR AND
JANICE
LANDRY—the
weekend anchor
team in the
nineties.

Miramichi to Bathurst. It's a geographically huge beat that requires a great deal of travel but tends to produce a lot of news and a lot of experience for those who tackle it. Among Farguson's predecessors is Andy Leblanc, now assistant news director and assignment editor for ATV. Andy parlayed his way from the North shore (in the days when the bureau was in Bathurst) to a reporting position in Fredericton before becoming ATV's Saint John based news director in the late-eighties. He later relocated to his hometown of Moncton before being promoted and transferred to the Halifax newsroom, where he's now "second in command."

Other northeastern New Brunswick alumni include: Marc Patrone, who's become one of the station's senior reporters covering politics in Halifax (and writing and recording music in his off hours); Newfoundland native Peter Ryan, who worked in the Sydney station before accepting a desk job at a private station in Ottawa; and Pat Foran, now consumer reporter at CTV flagship station CFTO in Toronto.

Charlottetown's daily newspaper, *The Guardian*, is well known for its masthead promise to "Cover the Island like the Dew." But when it comes to television, nobody covers PEI

PETER MALLETTE   BRUCE FRISKO

like Dan Viau, and he's all by himself competing against an entire CBC station. It's not unusual to see Dan arrive at a news event with just seconds to spare, carrying a camera, lights, tripod, and tape. If Dan doesn't know everyone on Prince Edward Island, almost everyone knows Dan. And in Nova Scotia's Pictou County, almost everyone knows the other Dan, New Glasgow native Dan MacIntosh. He covers northern and eastern Nova Scotia and has done so since graduating from St. F.X. longer ago than you would think, given his eternally youthful appearance. Dan has distinguished himself as a reporter on many occasions over the years and was the Atlantic Journalism Awards "Journalist of the Year" in 1989.

Randy MacDonald was a well-established reporter at CTV Ottawa station CJOH when he was lured home to Cape Breton in the eighties. Randy broke into television at CJCH-TV in Halifax a decade earlier, and is now ATV's senior reporter in Sydney.

Paul Pickrem was a cameraman and editor in the Halifax newsroom before moving to Cape Breton as a reporter/videographer. He's the first ATV technician to jump to the other side

CHRISTINE
HOLTORF AND
GREG CAMPBELL
juggling cameras
and satellite
feeds.

of the camera, although many of our reporters shoot their own material. Videography (the practice of having the person who operates the camera also appear in front of it) was a novelty in the eighties and nineties but is now an industry norm, particularly in smaller newsrooms. One of the truly regrettable consequences of the move to videography, has been the loss of some tremendously talented cameramen.

Two former ATV News employees are now members of the Nova Scotia legislature. Dave Wilson reported from Saint John in the late seventies but became famous in Cape Breton as the host of CJCB Radio's long running *Talkback* phone-in show. He was elected to the legislature as a Liberal MLA for Cape Breton East in a by-election in 1998. He was re-elected in the 1999 general election and then un-elected when voting irregularities forced another vote. He won the subsequent by-election, becoming the only Nova Scotia MLA to fight three elections in just over a year.

Frank Corbett was a veteran cameraman at ATV Sydney when he ran for the NDP and won a seat in the legislature. Corbett is an experienced labour leader who brings considerable passion to legislative debates.

The Other Side of the Camera

IN CANADIAN BROADCASTING, it is no secret that ATV has some of the best "shooters" in the business. Many have worked in larger television markets, but they often choose to return to the Maritimes for lifestyle reasons, although they remain in great demand for any national productions that come this way. It is also widely agreed that ATV has just about the best "live" technical staff in the country. That's because ATV does more live television both inside and outside the studio than just about any other station in the country. It is no exaggeration to say that *Live at 5* and the *ATV Evening News* have originated live from practically every city and town in the Maritimes. Our technicians routinely perform miracles, doing in minutes what it would take less experienced staff hours to do.

One of the reasons for this success is that the people who manage ATV's technical staff are former technicians who don't mind getting their hands dirty. Former operations manager Larry Wartman worked his way up from a junior staff position at his hometown TV station in Moncton. In the early days of *Live at 5* remotes, Larry was one of the guys running the cables.

John Silver, a master of television lighting technique, was one of two studio crew chiefs, and remained with ATV in a senior role in Larry Wartman's department. Greg Campbell, ATV's technical supervisor, is also a veteran of TV trench warfare. A former cameraman, he moved up through the ranks of the technical staff, heading the other studio crew. He was promoted further when Donnie Verge left ATV as part of what became known as the MITV "exodus of 88." Greg specializes in doing the impossible: finding ways out of tricky situations at a reasonable cost. During the station's coverage from London following the death of the Princess of Wales, Greg spent most of his time choreographing intricate satellite feeds, a cell phone jammed between a shoulder and one ear, and a conventional phoned pressed to the other. Then, and on countless other occasions, he expertly maneuvered his way around time zones and through currency conversions, buying time on various "birds" (satellites) at so many hours Zulu and so many pounds per minute. Greg is cool under pressure, which is fortunate for him because he's under pressure almost all the time.

Some of ATV's most seasoned and skilled technical people are veterans of the Campbell and Silver studio crews. The unshakable Dale Waterhouse is one of the best switchers in the business (a switcher is the person who manually executes the shots and visual effects called for by the director on a large panel also known as a switcher). He plays the switcher with the ease and grace of a concert pianist performing an intricate concerto.

ATV credit-watchers will have seen the name "Soupie" Campbell roll by at the end of shows like *Wonder Why? Up Home Tonight, Joan Kennedy,* and *The Andy Winters Show.* (Andy, by the way, was the alter ego of long-time ATV production manager Andy Coburn.) A top-notch editor, Soupie Campbell, along with another seasoned pro named Dave Peverill, has had a hand in creating virtually all of the videotaped programmes and commercials made "on tape" at ATV.

Although a considerable team effort, producing local television is not always as labour intensive as some people believe. The Hollywood image of huge technical crews and numerous takes of each shot simply does not apply. Most of ATV's commercials, for

ATV's
CAMERAPEOPLE
are widely
regarded as the
best in the
business.

example, often involve only cameraman Steve Townsend, a producer, occasionally an assistant, and a post-production editor.

Up Home Tonight was a weekly kitchen party shot in ATV's second studio. The brainchild of ATV producer Barry Bramhill and the show's brilliant host, Gordon Stobbe, it showcased homegrown Maritime talent long before the Celtic wave washed over the charts. Young performers named Natalie MacMaster, Ashley MacIsaac, the Rankins, and the Barra MacNeils got their start on Gordon Stobbe's knee "in the old kitchen." The set was so realistic some viewers thought it was actually Gordon Stobbe's house; when fire struck his real home, some viewers worried for the future of "Up Home." Fortunately, he and the show carried on, without injury.

Other young performers got their TV break on ATV programmes like *Up & Coming* and ASN's *New Faces*. Penny MacAulay put her special perspective as a talented performer to very good use behind the scenes as a producer of many of those shows. Grant Kennedy, Penny's audio engineer on many of those programmes, is now her husband. Grant is the same clever and enterprising soul who "hid" microphones in flowerpots and woodpiles all over the *Up Home Tonight* set so as not to destroy the look and feel of the

Veteran ATV
Switcher Dale
Waterhouse.

country kitchen! Another veteran ATV producer, Sharon Stiebel, could easily have had a career in opera had she not pursued television instead.

Audio engineers Jim Crook, Brian Norman, and Dave Eisner have played a crucial role in countless musical productions at the station. Camerapeople Gary Campbell, Paul Creelman, Kevin Doyle, Donnie Gaudet, Jim Hill, Jr., Greg Irvine, Jody Jessome, Keith Johns, Pat Kennedy, Sandra Kipis, Jim Kvammen, Cyril Lunney, Dave Pike, Carl Pomeroy, and Cyril Worth have been involved in dozens of productions, ranging from dramas to Paul Mennier's 1980s bowling series (co-hosted by Bruce Stephen). Technical producers John Colyer, John MacKinley, and Jeff Oakley are veterans of thousands of hours of live television, as are versatile technicians "JW" John Campbell, Ron Comstock, Dave Ead, Scott Innis, and Pernell Verhaeghe. A skilful and clever carpenter named Denny Saulnier built most of the sets and keeps the existing ones from falling apart!

Over the years, Leona Coburn produced a good many of those shows. As Leona Leblanc, she was well known to ATV viewers as host of many excellent local programmes and a wacky little 1970s game show called *Amca Cash Squares* (sponsored, logically enough, by Amca Food Brokers). Moncton-based Borden Macdonald hosted "The K-Mart Winners Circle" contest, in which viewers' names

PRODUCER LEONA
COBURN. As
Leona Leblanc,
she was a well-
known television
personality in the
seventies.

were drawn from a drum and attached to the names of the horses running in a prerecorded race at Montreal's Blue Bonnets raceway. There were prizes for win, place, and show. Borden also hosted a kids' show called *The Lobster Trap* in the early seventies on CKCW Moncton.

In Halifax, kids watched and appeared on a homegrown show called *Firehouse Frolics,* hosted by a venerable broadcaster named Murray McIvor, fondly and widely remembered as Fire Chief Murray. Many long-time ATV employees got their start on "Frolics," including tape-editor Art Steeves, whose considerable patience was often tested by a greenhorn named Steve Murphy! Art started as a microphone boom operator on "Frolics," and worked on *Live at 5* and the *ATV Evening News* from the day they debuted, until his retirement in 1999. Although they were best of friends and long-time colleagues, Dave Wright could never seem to remember Art's name...or anyone else's. Dave usually called the male members of the new staff by one of two nicknames—"Ace" or "Shooter." Art was "Arnie" on more than one occasion. The man who now does videotape editing for the evening news is sometimes called Maddog, although usually he's Victor (Cormier).

DIRECTOR
JOCELYN MURPHY
(right) and
production
assistant Dawn
Veinotte, who
has worked on
Live at 5 longer
than anyone else.

CAMERAMAN
GREG IRVINE
volunteering on
an early eighties
Christmas
Daddies show.

Carmella Gillis, who does the same job for Ron and Nancy on *Live at 5,* is "Carm" and (for those who've known her the longest) "Gillyguts." She's a member of the Gillis clan of North Sydney, which also includes long-time New Brunswick radio personality Sandy Gillis and his alter ego "Jimmy-the-Janitor."

Behind the news cameras, in the days before "videography," Pat Richard and Shawn DeLong were fixtures in the New Brunswick legislature press gallery. Their political contacts in government were at least as numerous and as reliable as most reporters'. Brian Chisholm, Mike Burchill, and Murray Titus were all raised in Saint John and know the city like the back of their hands. Only Brian is still "shooting news" for ATV. Murray has assumed a management role at CTV's Vancouver television station and Mike is a successful freelance cameraman who still turns up on many ATV remote broadcasts. And so does Paul MacEachern, who, with Dave Stewart, was a stalwart in the Moncton newsroom. Darryl Reeves is the old hand in Sydney. His younger brother George has made a successful move to ATV News in Halifax, as has another Cape Breton veteran, Stuart MacDougall. Both are news cameramen. Bruce Hennessey, Gary Mansfield, and the late Ken Betts spent many years behind the lens in Sydney under the leadership of Sonny McTavish, who became station manager when Ken Boyce retired.

These days, when I acknowledge "my colleagues on both sides of the camera," I am speaking specifically of several people who work on *The ATV Evening News* everyday. Producer Wade Keller was a videographer for MITV during the Westray mine disaster. Both his work and his work ethic greatly impressed Mark Campbell, who promptly hired Wade as a production assistant. After rising to the position of director of the evening news, Wade joined *CBC Newsworld* briefly in the late nineties. He returned to ATV just in time to launch the one-hour *ATV Evening News* in May 2000. Julie Caswell now brings her considerable anchoring and reporting experience to a producing role.

Dartmouth-native Leo Carter came to ATV news as an auto-cue or teleprompt operator directly from Atlantic Media Institute (AMI). Former owner and instructor Alex J. Walling says Leo was one of the best students and hardest workers to come out of the

CAMERAMAN PAT
KENNEDY (left)
dons the armour
that helps control
the hand-held,
hydraulic
steadicam, which
allows for
smooth
movement
around the
newsroom. Floor
Director Kirk
Neff assists.

school. (That's high praise from a man with a Trojan work ethic and who, as a francophone kid growing up in Quebec City, taught himself English and went on to a successful broadcasting career in English television and radio.) Leo is a production assistant on *The ATV Evening News,* and director of Bruce Frisko's *ATV News Nightside.* Another AMI alumni, Moncton's Derek Haggett, was working in the same role before he accepted a similar position at the mother ship, CFTO Toronto, flagship of the CTV Television Network.

Heather Macaulay cut her teeth in television at Shaw Cable in Lower Sackville, Nova Scotia. She was recruited by Jocelyn Murphy for the launch of *Breakfast Television* and was the show's first floor director (the person who oversees the programme in the studio, giving hosts time cues, moving guests around, and communicating with the director in the control room). These days, Heather is sitting in the *Live at 5* producer's chair and Jocelyn is calling the shots as director of both *Live at 5* and *The ATV Evening News.*

At their side in the control room each night is a woman who's been "behind the scenes" on *Live at 5* longer than anyone else. Dawn Veinotte-Mosher was producing Dave Wright's *Hotline* radio show when he made the move to full-time television in 1981. It wasn't long before Dave lured Dawn to the bright lights of the TV studio. Dawn has produced hundreds of segments for *Live at 5*, particularly for Dr. Stewart Cameron and now with Dr. A.J. She also presides over the giant accordion files that contain the "Marriage Milestones" and oversees the process that leads to the selection of "The Maritimer of the Week."

And there are others…many others who, in some way or another, have made possible what appears on the TV set every night. Graphic designers like Jack Dowell, Dave Goudge, Greg O'Sullivan, and Guy Boucher are the creative minds and artists who've designed the various *Live at 5* logos (there have been five over the years), the openings, and animations and graphics. There are the electronics engineers, who literally keep the television stations on the air (and in TV, the equipment is always a "breaking story"): Wally Robert, Don Edgar, John Jay, Bob Zeidler, Dennis Disque, Gary Robertson, Carson McDavid, Ed Bennett, and many others who have worked with and for them. During the long days on the road with "Celebrate the Maritimes," we jokingly referred to the engineers as "blacksmiths." Then one day, one of them pointed out that if they were shoeing horses that made us…the horses!

Closing Credits

MUCH OF THE CREDIT FOR THE ENDURING SUCCESS of *Live at 5* lies on the other side of the TV set. Viewers have always played an important supporting role. The programme was born in response to the overwhelming support of its predecessor, Dave Wright's *Notebook,* and in the years since has relied on viewer suggestions for some of its most successful features and stories.

The "Adopt-a-Village" campaign of the mid-eighties would not have succeeded without the tremendous outpouring of support from people across the Maritimes. And it was viewers who propelled "Celebrate the Maritimes" into communities across the three provinces. Over the years, tens of thousands of Maritimers have taken part in *Live at 5* telephone polls and photo contests. Hundreds have nominated "Maritimers of the Week" and dozens wear "Maritimer of the Week" pins. Thousands more have been featured in the milestones segments. The telephone, mail, and internet are steady sources of story ideas, which come, for the most part, from people who expect to see their neighbours, family, friends, or maybe even themselves on *Live at 5*.

Over the years, hundreds of people I have never seen before have walked up to me on the street, in malls, doctors' offices, restaurants, and movie theatres, and said, "I feel like I know you." Every other member of the ATV News *Live at 5* team speaks of similar experiences. We have received birthday and Christmas cards (some containing cash, which goes to charity) and gifts from viewers; good wishes on the births of our children and questions about them from people who've kept track of their ages (my daughter Nora is fourteen, my son Brendan is four).

Most significantly, the people who've watched us on television for all these years feel a sense of ownership towards the programme. We have been made welcome in every city and town in the Maritimes by people who accept us into their homes every night. Jocelyn and I have never gone anywhere in the world that we haven't met someone "from home." In the Paris-Nord train station, it was people from Dartmouth. A few years later, in London's famed Westminster Abbey, a woman in a pew behind us tapped me on the shoulder and whispered, "Steve Murphy! What are you doing here?" She was from Prince Edward Island. Browsing through the linens and crystal in the House of Dublin on Nassau Street in Dublin, Ireland, we once encountered a bus tour full of Maritimers. The clerks were more than perplexed after I signed a few autographs. As Jocelyn and I rang in a few purchases one of the clerks finally mustered up the curiosity to ask, "I'm sorry sir, but who are you?"

But my most amazing encounter with an ATV viewer occurred not in a large city, but in rural Ireland. It took almost an hour for my cousin Sean Elmore to drive us from the medieval town of Carlingford, where he and his wife Rita live, to historic Mellifont Abbey—at the end of a dirt path, off a seldom-travelled country road, off a secondary highway. Almost in the middle of a farmer's field, it was truly in the middle of nowhere. When we arrived at the impressive ruins of the twelfth-century Cistercian monastery, there was only one other car in the gravel parking lot. Sean stayed behind in the car while Jocelyn and I made our way to the Bord Failte information kiosk, where for a modest ten pence visitors could obtain a leaflet outlining the history of the abbey. Imagine our surprise when the people in the queue ahead of us, the only other tourists on the property, spun around and shrieked, "Oh my God!" They knew me from *Live at 5* and recognized Jocelyn from *Breakfast Television*! They were from Miramichi. Back at the car, Sean Elmore asked whether we knew "those people." When we explained that they were viewers from the Maritimes, Sean quipped, "You must be the most famous man in Canada!" Not even close I explained, but the coincidence was both amusing and amazing.

Here at home, scarcely a day goes by that a viewer doesn't say something nice. Oh sure, sometimes it's something not so nice, but that's been the exception. Nancy, Ron, Peter, and Starr all have similar stories. The special and rare relationship between the people on the show and the people watching it is the real reason for its longevity and success. And so, for my colleagues on both sides of our cameras, thank you for being such an important part of life at five. We'll see you tomorrow night.

Postscript

LIVE AT 5 VIEWERS HAVE LONG MEMORIES. I am often asked about the people who've played a role on the programme over the years. It usually begins with, "What ever happened to ?......" So here is an update on former *Live at 5* personalities.

A casualty in one of the interminable rounds of layoffs at CBC, Yvonne Colbert is now a consumer affairs advisor with the Nova Scotia Power Corporation.

After a successful term as chair of the Nova Scotia Advisory Council on the Status of Women, Debi Forsyth-Smith was appointed to the Nova Scotia Cabinet of Premier Donald Cameron. She failed to win a seat in the legislature and after working for the PC caucus launched a career in public relations.

Bruce Graham gave up the anchor chair and is now semi-retired and living outside of Halifax. He ran for the leadership of the Nova Scotia Liberal Party and recently published a novel, *The Parrsboro Boxing Club*. He's always been proud of Parrsboro!

After several years anchoring the evening news with Bruce Graham on MITV (later Global), Laura Lee Langley is now a senior public affairs official with the Nova Scotia Government.

Bill MacKay is pursuing a successful career in the insurance industry.

After two years as anchor and interim news director at VTV Vancouver, Paul Mennier is anchoring the evening news on A-Channel, an independent station in Edmonton.

Ian Morrison rose to the position of executive producer of ATV News before reuniting with Dick Prat as executive producer at CHCH Hamilton. He is now in news management at CHUM's CFPL (The New PL) in London, Ontario.

After several years in television programming, Dick Prat briefly returned to news management in Hamilton, and is now network scheduler for Maple Leafs Television in Toronto.

Kelly Ryan reported for MITV and is now a well-respected national reporter for CBC Radio.

Harris Sullivan dabbles in broadcast and media consulting.

Steve Weagle is chief meteorologist at the NBC affiliate in West Palm Beach Florida.

An independent producer of children's programmes, Richard Zurawski is educating yet another generation of kids in reruns of *Wonder Why?*

And Dave Wright? He is happily and healthily retired in the Barrie, Ontario, area. He spends some time in Florida. Apart from an occasional stint on radio in Barrie, he's out of the media, but did graciously agree to write the foreword for this book. Thanks again, Boomer.